From Words to Wisdom

From Words to Wisdom

Supporting Academic Language Use in PreK–3rd Grade

Erica M. Barnes
Jill F. Grifenhagen
David K. Dickinson

Foreword by Susan B. Neuman

TEACHERS COLLEGE PRESS

TEACHERS COLLEGE | COLUMBIA UNIVERSITY
NEW YORK AND LONDON

Published by Teachers College Press,® 1234 Amsterdam Avenue, New York, NY 10027

Copyright © 2021 by Teachers College, Columbia University

Front cover by Rebecca Lown Design; photo by WavebreakmediaMicro/ Adobe Stock.

Library of Congress Cataloging-in-Publication Data

Names: Barnes, Erica Marie, author. | Grifenhagen, Jill Freiberg, author. | Dickinson, David K., author.
Title: From words to wisdom : supporting academic language use in preK-3rd grade / Erica M. Barnes, Jill F. Grifenhagen, David K. Dickinson.
Other titles: Supporting academic language use in preKindergarten-third grade
Description: New York : Teachers College Press, [2021] | Series: Language and Literacy Series | Includes bibliographical references and index.
Identifiers: LCCN 2021015282 (print) | LCCN 2021015283 (ebook) | ISBN 9780807765876 (Paperback : acid-free paper) | ISBN 9780807765883 (Hardcover : acid-free paper) | ISBN 9780807779835 (eBook)
Subjects: LCSH: Language arts (Early childhood)—United States. | Academic language—Study and teaching—United States. | Teachers—Training of.
Classification: LCC LB1139.5.L35 .B37 2021 (print) | LCC LB1139.5.L35 (ebook) | DDC 372.6/044—dc23
LC record available at https://lccn.loc.gov/2021015282
LC ebook record available at https://lccn.loc.gov/2021015283

ISBN 978-0-8077-6587-6 (paper)
ISBN 978-0-8077-6588-3 (hardcover)
ISBN 978-0-8077-7983-5 (ebook)

Printed on acid-free paper
Manufactured in the United States of America

Contents

Foreword

What IS academic language? How does it differ from casual talk? Why is it important? And, if so, how do I teach it, especially to young children? These are only some of the questions you might hear when considering the term *academic language*. The term itself seems vague—it's hard to get a handle on its meaning, and even harder to relate it to language development for children in the early years of schooling.

Yet at the same time we also know that the first 4 years of children's lives represent a period of astonishing growth in language and the ability to acquire new words, syntax, and semantic knowledge. Therefore, think about the opportunities to acquire new and additional language registers when children are so eager to learn. Just watch as they play with their friends and family: They'll imitate many of the behaviors they see using the mannerisms and speech patterns of adults. In these acts, they are conveying their desire to act "grown up," to acquire the more specialized language patterns from those adults closest to them in different contextualized settings.

But unlike the casual conversations that children will often emulate, acquiring the register of academic language is not something learned through daily discourse. It needs to be taught. As Barnes, Grifenhagen, and Dickinson so deftly describe, academic language is a specialized register associated with conveying content knowledge. It is the difference between having a conversation with a friend where both of you might share a history and talk in relative short-cuts, to one in where you might be introducing a more technical subject to colleagues unfamiliar with a topic. In these latter situations, there is likely to be a higher density of concepts, with words that may have more precise and contextualized meaning with referents not in the here-and-now.

These authors demystify the topic of academic language by showing us visually through tables, graphs, and examples how this register differs from colloquial language. They not only tell but show us how the features, grammar, and context of academic language may work, and how to foster it in our teaching. Throughout my reading, I kept thinking, "hey, I could do this," with the ideas clearly described in such a way that one could immediately implement them in classrooms the next day. These are powerful instructional techniques that take the complexities of academic language and make them actionable.

But the authors also recognize that the building of academic language is not merely a set of instructional techniques or add-ons to existing practices. Rather, it is a feature of instruction that must be integrated in everything we do with children: in our conversations at mealtime, our discussion formats, our science and math activities, and our sharing time with classroom friends. It requires us to be more intentional in our use of language with children and to support their ability to communicate their thoughts with others.

For children are great imitators. They will learn by observing and imitating the adults they most admire. Imitation can be a great accelerator of learning. Therefore, when teachers teach and use academic language in their teaching, children are likely to try it out. They won't merely duplicate what they hear but will become increasingly sensitive to the register in which ideas are conveyed. In this respect, this book is about and for teachers. In promoting academic language, teachers are mentoring young children, helping to build a foundation for their students to communicate their ideas among a community of learners.

Some might question whether academic language should be taught so early on, starting in preschool and beyond in elementary school. Isn't it all too academic? Aren't we rushing children's development when they should be at play? Yet think of academic language like this: The child is eager to share the news about the chicks that just hatched in his classroom's incubator. He's been observing their activity day-by-day, tasked by his teacher to check on the temperature and humidity in the incubator, and to turn the eggs carefully three times a day. As he arrives in class one morning, he hears quiet chirping sounds, and quickly knows it's *the* day. During sharing time he'll want to share his discoveries and growing expertise by telling his friends about his discoveries and the caring and feeding of these tired little chicks. With his teacher's support in so doing, he's likely to talk like a scientist using the register of academic language. Of special note, academic language is not the end goal here; rather, it is the means to most effectively convey his scientific ideas with others.

And this is the stance that threads throughout the book. Academic language is useful to students in the long term, not just something that is learned and then lost. It is an enabler, helping young children expand their ideas and communicate with others. The authors have done a brilliant job of highlighting the latest research on language and detailing the complexities of academic language while making it clear and easy to understand. In reading this text, educators will develop a deeper knowledge base about language in general, as well as academic language in particular. In re-reading the text, they will increasingly incorporate many of the recommendations throughout the book in their daily teaching. It will increasingly become a natural and most necessary part of the instructional program.

Through examples of daily instructional practices and teacher-child interactions, the authors make a powerful case that developing academic language is not for the few, but for all our children. Multilingual learners, those learning a new language, are highly capable of developing an additional language register to their already existing skills. But there is not a moment to wait. Children are natural socializers, eager to share their ideas with others. Give them an additional set of tools and they will use them in developing their knowledge network. It will not happen overnight, however. Shifts from more casual to more academic language need to start early, when habits are just forming, and can become increasingly routine in daily practice.

By making a case for academic language, these authors are helping us all open a gateway for children to become members of a language community highly valued in school learning. It may become one of the most prized assets that we can give to our young children.

—Susan B. Neuman

Preface
Learning the Language of School

Children are asked to learn many things when they arrive in early childhood classrooms. They learn how to get along well with others, follow rules and routines, acquire content area information, and meet adults' expectations. Underlying all of this learning is language. Young children arrive in school having not yet achieved adult-like competence with all language rules and routines, but most are relatively proficient in casual conversation with peers and familiar adults. They have learned how to interact linguistically with others from engaging with family and friends and have intuitively derived the linguistic rules and routines of their community. This acquisition comes from years of observation and engagement as children are enculturated in their linguistic communities through face-to-face interactions with mature speakers (Tomasello, 2000).

Language is the foundation upon which academic skills are built. Children with strong language skills tend to perform well in school, as they are able to access the instructed content. Children who are less familiar with the language of instruction must overcome the additional obstacle of learning the language of instruction in addition to the instructed content. While this issue is well-documented for children who are English language learners, less attention has been devoted to the language-learning needs of native English speakers from a variety of backgrounds. Many families use a casual, informal linguistic style at home, and many families speak a dialect that differs from classroom language. These out-of-school linguistic practices do not always align with the language practices of classrooms, which commonly feature academic language (Schleppegrell, 2004). The degree of match between a child's home dialect and academic language may factor heavily into the child's access to the instructed curriculum.

Academic language is the language used for completing academic tasks in the content areas of school (Bunch, 2013; Chamot & O'Malley, 1994). Academic language is a register, which is a type of talk particular to a specific setting that is shaped by the relationships among the participants and the content of the interaction (Dickinson et al., 2014). In other words, registers are the patterns of talk that reflect the *participants, places*, and *purpose* of the interaction. Registers include vocabulary, syntax, and discourse.

These bundles of linguistic capacities are deployed in slightly different ways in different contexts. Children employ the registers they have acquired as they understand oral or written language. However, there may be substantial differences between the registers they have acquired and those needed to understand and produce spoken and written language in classrooms. These discrepancies may create difficulties in understanding and producing the language expected of them in classrooms. Therefore, students who have not yet mastered academic language may struggle to read academic texts, engage in academic discussions, and write using academic language.

When children have not yet been exposed to academic language in sufficient doses, they may face some challenges in understanding and acquiring classroom language and literacy practices (Cazden, 2002; Fang, 2006; Heath, 1983, 2012; Moje et al., 2000). In particular, children from minoritized linguistic communities are more likely to have greater differences between their home languages and the language of the classroom (Heath, 2012; Mancilla-Martinez & Lesaux, 2010; Reardon et al., 2012). This does not mean that children are linguistically deficient, but rather that the home registers they speak are quite different from an academic register. Likewise, it does not mean any children are incapable of becoming conversant in an academic register, but rather that they have *yet* to learn an academic register. All children will require some degree of support in acquiring an academic register, particularly as they approach complex texts in academic disciplines.

Acquiring academic language is of great importance as it is the gateway into the instructional content valued in classrooms. Students' knowledge of academic language is related to their academic success as those with more experience with speaking and hearing academic language tend to experience greater academic success (Nagy & Townsend, 2012; Schleppegrell, 2004). Importantly, students' knowledge of academic language plays a critical role in reading comprehension, such that students with greater knowledge of academic language tend to have a better understanding of the complex texts they read (Uccelli et al., 2015a).

How we talk is a central part of who we are, and it can require great effort to shift our language practices, which become routinized over time. This is not to say that it is impossible to learn a new register, but rather that care and attention must be applied in order for the desired outcome to be achieved. Being explicit about the differences between registers is critical, as is having the learner be engaged in the learning process. This is of particular importance when the new register is distinctly different from one's home register. We cannot expect all students to learn an academic register without explicit instruction.

Because so much effort and time are needed, it is essential to begin apprenticing young children into academic language at an early age. The last 10 years have brought about multiple waves of educational standards, all of which address the importance of academic language from the earliest years of schooling. The adoptions of the Common Core State Standards, Next Generation Science Standards, and the C3 Social Studies standards have placed stronger emphasis on content-area instruction in earlier grades, with this content couched in academic language. Specifically, the standards call for instruction that assists students with understanding complex texts and their academic language. Some sets of standards include specific glossaries of academic vocabulary, as well as goals for the inclusion of appropriate tone, stance, and complex syntax, all of which are elements of academic language. These features of academic language may require specific instruction, particularly for those students less familiar with classroom discourse.

Teacher credentialing programs have taken heed of the shifts in standards, with some teacher credentialing assessments evaluating prospective teachers on their knowledge of and ability to teach from and with academic language. The Teacher Performance Assessment (edTPA), an assessment linked to many states' credentialing programs, assesses prospective teachers on their abilities to identify and support the academic vocabulary and language demands (syntax or discourse) of their submitted lesson plans. Prospective teachers are asked to consider word-, sentence-, and discourse-level features of instruction and how these features may impact student language and content knowledge development.

Additionally, current and potential changes in policy regarding early childhood education indicate a potential increase in student enrollment in prekindergarten and kindergarten programs. As of 2018, nearly 84% of 5-year-olds, 68% of 4-year-olds, and 40% of 3-year-olds were enrolled in preprimary classrooms, a trend that has remained relatively stable over the last 10 years (NCES). Many cities and states are now contemplating the possibility of making prekindergarten and kindergarten either free or mandatory, which may cause a sharp rise in enrollment. This means there is a need for more well-prepared early childhood teachers than ever, and these teachers will serve an increasingly linguistically diverse population of children.

Each of these factors indicate a need for developing the knowledge and instructional base of early childhood and early primary teachers, who serve as the foundation for launching children's educational careers and future success. Our collective years of experience working with novice and veteran teachers has shown us the pervasive need for helping teachers learn more about academic language and how to build classroom engagements that support young children's acquisition of this register. Academic language has primarily been addressed and studied at the upper elementary through college levels, with scant attention paid to early childhood settings. Our combined scholarship has been at the forefront of examining an academic register in early childhood classrooms.

In spite of the relative importance of academic language, teachers may not be well-versed in its components or how to teach children about academic language while simultaneously honoring the language that children bring with them to the classroom. Teachers should become language conscious themselves in order to instill this in their students. This language consciousness should begin with an awareness of academic language, such that teachers are able to identify its features and have knowledge of how academic language may vary by academic discipline. Knowledge of academic language lays the foundation for building pedagogical skills for teaching with and about academic language in a manner that helps children become language conscious themselves. This text seeks to empower teachers to become conscious of the differences in language, appreciate the affordances of different types of language for different circumstances, and assist them with teaching young children about and with academic language.

In this book, we'll discuss ways to identify, teach, and expand on academic language across the school day in early childhood and elementary settings. We begin in Chapter 1 by providing a broad overview of academic language to acquaint the reader with this multifaceted and complex topic. In Chapter 2, we briefly describe how children learn language by describing principles of language learning and how to facilitate language growth. Chapter 3 addresses linguistic diversity through the lens of registers, which celebrate diversity while fostering academic language. Chapters 4, 5, and 6 address academic vocabulary, complex syntax, and academic discourse. Each chapter explains the key features of the associated level of academic language, while also providing general strategies and guidance for instruction.

Chapters 7 through 10 address how academic language may be facilitated in different classroom settings. Our research has found that teachers naturally vary in their register use across the day, such that some settings yield higher amounts of academic vocabulary than others, while other settings are richer in complex syntax and academic content (Dickinson et al., 2014). Given these differences based on instructional setting, we review each setting or content area individually in a way that naturally leverages the strength of each. This setting-by-setting approach also allows you to try out different strategies one setting at a time, gradually adopting an academic language stance. Chapter 7 addresses the nonacademic settings of mealtimes and sharing time, both of which are ripe opportunities for fostering academic language given their emphasis on decontextualized talk. Chapter 8 investigates playful learning. It includes ideas for teaching about and with academic language through game play, music, and dramatic play. Chapter 9 describes scientific language and how this register varies from other academic disciplines, with an emphasis on project-based learning that encourages students to communicate like scientists. Mathematical language is addressed in Chapter 10. Ideas for teaching mathematical vocabulary and argumentation are presented.

Chapter 11 addresses assessing academic language. This practical chapter provides assessment ideas for monitoring and marking student growth in academic language, as well as tools for assessing the classroom environment and supports for academic language. Checklists, assessment ideas, and observational protocols are provided. Our appendices provide checklists for observing academic language in mathematics and science specifically, a general academic language observation tool, and an assessment for academic language implementation. Additionally, we provide digital resources and a list of children's literature for building academic language.

Our research shows that even small changes can make a big difference in children's language development (Barnes & Dickinson, 2017; Dickinson & Porche, 2011), so make sure to move at a pace that works best for you and your students. In fact, we recommend starting small and trying out strategies for only one setting at a time. As you become more comfortable, you can take on different settings and gradually build up your repertoire. Remember, children acquire language slowly over an extended period of time, so make sure to give yourself the time that you need too.

Acknowledgments

We are grateful for the support provided by the following grants that aided with the development, evaluation, and inspiration for this text: #R324E060088; #R305T990312-00, #REC-9979948, #R305A110128, and #R305A150432L.

CHAPTER 1

An Overview of Academic Language

> **PRIMING QUESTIONS:**
> 1. What is academic language and how does it differ from casual talk? What are the features of academic language?
> 2. Why is academic language important for academic performance? Why should instruction begin at the early childhood level?

In this introductory chapter, we will briefly describe the components of academic language and how these components are associated with children's later academic success. Later chapters will provide richer descriptions of each component along with instructional strategies and materials for teaching and integrating academic language across a variety of settings in prekindergarten through 3rd-grade classrooms.

ACADEMIC OR CASUAL LANGUAGE?

To more clearly understand academic language, it is helpful to distinguish what is *not* academic language. Bailey and Butler (2003) indicate that academic language stands in contrast to the informal everyday speech register that students use outside of the classroom as they differ in terms of emphasis on explicitness, precision, abstraction, and formality (van Kleeck, 2015). Casual (informal) and academic registers lie on a continuum, such that each end of the spectrum may contain similar elements, but in different amounts. At one end of the continuum is casual language, which is the language of the home or social settings. An important function of this language is to establish or maintain social relationships (see Figure 1.1). It contains common vocabulary that is largely known and understood by the speakers, with limited use of complex syntax due to the contextualized nature and shared understanding of the discussions. This language has a casual tone where the speakers seek to share experiences. Neither participant dictates the conversation unless it is agreed upon by the speakers because the participants share similar status in the discussion.

Figure 1.1. The Continuum of Casual to Academic Language

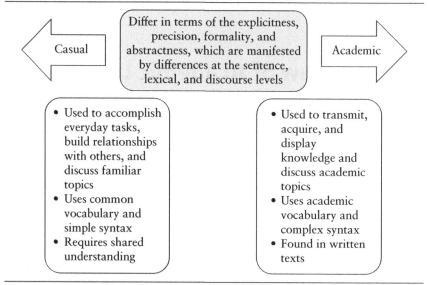

Source: Adapted from van Kleeck (2014, 2015).

Casual conversation serves to accomplish everyday tasks, which frequently involve discussing social interactions or engagements. The following example of casual conversation occurred in a Head Start prekindergarten classroom when the teacher was engaging a student at the block center (all names are pseudonyms). Notice the topic of conversation, the degree of familiarity among the speakers, the type of syntax and vocabulary employed, and the back-and-forth nature of the dialogue.

> *Teacher:* What are you building?
> *Student:* A castle. Need another one. (Points to a rectangular block)
> *Teacher:* Here you go. Does the castle have a bridge?
> *Student:* Yes, there. (Points to spot on castle)
> *Teacher:* Oh, I see, there it is!

The discussion focuses on a topic of mutual interest, building with blocks during centers time. The teacher is asking a genuine question as she may not be able to identify the structure that the student is building. This type of genuine question is seeking out information with the goal of building a social relationship among the participants. The syntax is relatively simple, with most sentences containing simple subjects and verbs with little inclusion of descriptive language. Some utterances are not complete sentences (*yes, there*), as there is no need for the inclusion of a subject and verb. Instead, the student can simply point out the answer in the physical environment. There is a relative balance of talk between the participants, with neither taking a stance of expert or director of the conversation.

At the other end of the spectrum is academic language, which we define as the specialized oral or written language of academic settings associated with communicating understanding of disciplinary content (Barnes et al., 2016; Dickinson et al., 2014; Nagy & Townsend, 2012). Academic language consists of word-, sentence-, and discourse-level elements. At the word level, there is great diversity of vocabulary and relatively large amounts of academic vocabulary. Sentence-level features of academic language include complex syntax, such as lexically dense clauses and phrases that add precision. Discourse-level features refer to how written or spoken communication is constructed in ways that reflect the social context. Academic language emphasizes discipline-specific content (mathematics, social studies, and so on), privileges decontextualized topics, addresses different genres of communication (functions), and includes a formal tone that implies expertise. It is the combination of these features that makes academic language so rich, complex, and worthy of instruction (see the following list).

Features and Descriptions of Academic Language

Feature of Academic Language	Description
Academic Vocabulary	Technical or precise terms associated within or across specific academic disciplines. These terms are commonly found in academic textbooks but may be less common in casual conversation.
Complex Syntax	Syntax refers to the manner in which words are put together to form clauses or sentences. Complex syntax includes multiple syntactical features (see Table 1.2).
Tone and Stance	The degree of familiarity of topic or audience based on the context. May imply expertise or social standing.
Decontextualization	Talk that refers to something not in the immediate physical environment.
Genre	Specific form or type of discourse that serves a social function. Genres have distinguishing lexical and grammatical features.

Compare and contrast the following conversation featuring some elements of academic language with the earlier example of casual talk. Be sure to look for grammatical features, content-area knowledge and vocabulary, decontextualized topics, and formal tone.

> *Teacher:* We've talked about insects. We've talked about spiders. Now we're going to talk about birds. A duck is a type of what?
> *Sarah:* Bird.
> *Jonah:* He live in the water.
> *Teacher:* And how do birds travel?
> *Sarah:* They fly.
> *Teacher:* Some fly, and some do what?
> *Jonah:* Swim!
> *Teacher:* Some birds swim? Some of them move like we move. How do we move?
> *Sarah:* And some of them walk.
> *Teacher:* Some of them walk. Very good! Okay let's talk about the ones that fly. Can you all think of a bird that flies?
> *Jonah:* A yellow one. That's on that book right there.
> *Teacher:* What is a yellow bird called?
> *Teacher:* Canary.
> *Jonah:* Canary.
> *Teacher:* (spells) C-A-N-A-R-Y.

This conversation differs from the example of casual talk in the topic of discussion and how it is introduced. The teacher is guiding the conversation to the topic of instruction, birds and how they travel. She introduces this science-focused topic and asks students a closed-response question for which she is looking for a specific answer. This type of questioning practice implies expertise on behalf of the teacher as she dictates whether the response is correct or incorrect. The teacher is seeking to know if the children have the desired knowledge, which places her in the role of the expert. The teacher introduces academic vocabulary, *canary*, as she precisely names a specific bird the child is describing. Additionally, some descriptive phrases are included to provide greater clarity (*that flies, the ones that fly*) and increase the complexity of the syntax. The goal of this informative discussion is to build content area knowledge. It is important to note that, although academic language is often associated with printed material, oral interactions such as this can introduce children to its structure and patterns of use.

HOW MIGHT ACADEMIC LANGUAGE LOOK IN EARLY CHILDHOOD CLASSROOMS?

Examining the definitions and descriptions may have you wondering what role academic language could possibly play in a prekindergarten or early elementary setting. After all, academic language is about "literate language" (Snow, 1983), and very few children in the earliest years of schooling, if any, are fully literate in a conventional sense. But remember, academic language

Figure 1.2. Discourse-, Sentence-, and Word-Level Features of Academic Language

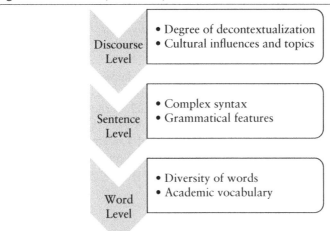

Discourse Level
- Degree of decontextualization
- Cultural influences and topics

Sentence Level
- Complex syntax
- Grammatical features

Word Level
- Diversity of words
- Academic vocabulary

falls on a continuum of communication complexity that ranges from very casual talk that could occur between a mother and infant to highly academic written arguments occurring between two Nobel Prize–winning physicists. The academic language of early childhood classrooms is simpler than the academic language found in college-level classrooms. However, in order for students to learn to use and understand challenging forms of academic language, they must first learn more simple versions. Nonetheless, all academic registers emphasize the conveyance of academic knowledge through specific word-, sentence-, and discourse-level choices (see Figure 1.2).

Consider what is deemed academic content in early childhood classrooms and how this might factor into developing your definition of academic language. Early childhood curricula frequently focus and build on academic topics that continue throughout formal schooling, such as science, social studies, reading and writing (literacy or English Language Arts), and mathematics. Of course, social studies in early childhood may not look or sound like high school social studies. Early childhood and elementary topics are precursors that help children build the knowledge and understanding required for later academic success. While one might be teaching about the American Revolution, the other might be talking about community workers and their jobs. Nonetheless, both are covering academic content with specific language and vocabulary associated with them. In high school, the students might be learning about the colonization of North America by a monarchy, while in pre-K or early elementary students might be learning about how firefighters help keep people safe. Both units of study are very important in terms of being an American citizen, but each contain unique vocabulary and topics. The vocabulary appropriate for teaching about the American Revolution (*monarchy, republic, militia*) would not be appropriate for teaching about firefighters (*extinguisher, hydrant, helmet*), and vice versa. Both lists of words contain academic vocabulary, as these are the words central to the academic topics.

Thus, even in early childhood classrooms, academic language contains academic vocabulary, complex syntax, and rigorous discourse. In the following sections, we provide a brief overview of each of these elements, with each being described at length in subsequent chapters. The following pages describe word, sentence, and discourse features of academic language from a functional grammar perspective, which emphasizes how each feature plays a specific role in the talk based on the involved places, purposes, and participants (Schleppegrell, 2004).

Word-Level Elements: Academic Vocabulary

Academic registers are characterized by academic vocabulary terms that allow for precision and accuracy. This precision is required as the topics of academic language tend to be removed from the present location (decontextualized), thus requiring the speakers to provide greater detail in order for the development of shared understanding among the participants.

The Common Core State Standards (CCSS) define academic vocabulary as words that may be content-specific or used across a variety of content areas to convey precise academic or disciplinary content (Conley, 2014). These words are not commonly found in casual conversation, but are frequently found in academic texts and materials. These words are of high value for understanding academic texts and are central to developing conceptual understanding of disciplinary content. Baumann and Graves (2010) lay out five organizing categories for academic vocabulary described in Table 1.1. Methods for identifying and selecting academic vocabulary for instruction are provided at length in Chapter 4.

Academic language is also marked by the diversity of words due to the precision needed to communicate content knowledge. Consider an informational text on wolves, and the amount and types of vocabulary words that may be included to discuss features of the wolves such as their diets, habitats, predation habits, and rates of extinction. Just discussing the diet could include rich vocabulary such as *deer, elk, caribou, moose,* and *bison*. Vocabulary can be viewed as a proxy for conceptual knowledge, such that a person who is an expert in a certain topic is more likely to know more words associated with that topic than another person who is a novice (Anderson & Freebody, 1981). People who are experts in a subject matter tend to have a large and diverse bank of words associated with that topic. Academic language conveys an expert stance, and it is essential to have a strong command of content-specific vocabulary.

Table 1.1. Categorizations of Academic Vocabulary

Category	Definition	Example
General academic	Terms that appear across a variety of disciplines, but the meanings of the terms may vary depending on the context	*Range* in mathematics (the span between numbers) and *range* in social studies (a range of mountains)
Domain-specific	Technical, precise, low-frequency words that are content specific and frequently appear in content-area texts but rarely outside the content area	*Filibuster, gastropod, Pi, symbolism, theme*
Literary	Terms used by authors (particularly of narratives) referring to the plot, setting, characters, and so on	*Serene, bucolic, tranquil*
Symbols	Graphics, mathematical notations, emoticons, icons, and charts that are present in written text and increasingly in digital media	+, =, @, %, &
Metalanguage	Literate language used to describe specific features of texts	*Glossary, index, table of contents*

Source: Adapted from Baumann and Graves (2010).

Sentence-Level Elements: Syntactic and Grammatical Features

Comprehension of oral or written language goes beyond understanding the meaning of individual words, as the reader/listener must use larger chunks of language such as clauses, sentences, and paragraphs to determine meaning (Share & Leikin, 2004; Storch & Whitehurst, 2002). For academic language to be understood, the reader/listener must be knowledgeable of how words and phrases are used to establish referents, connect ideas and thoughts, create cohesion, and organize concepts.

The organization and structure of academic language differs from conversational or casual language (Schleppegrell, 2004). This structure may be achieved through the inclusion of complex syntax, which refers to the degree of complexity in how sentences are composed of words from various grammatical categories (nouns, verbs, pronouns) and syntactic structures (clauses, phrases). Simply put, syntax is the set of rules used to organize words into more complex ideas using phrases, clauses, and sentences.

In this text, we take a functional linguistics approach to discussing syntax, discussing how clause-level elements are used in particular contexts (or

Table 1.2. Descriptions and Examples of Grammatical Features of Academic Language

Term and Definition	Example
Clause: A group of words containing a subject and a verb. An independent clause is a simple sentence. A dependent clause may begin with "although, since, if, when, because" and cannot stand on its own.	**Independent clause:** The cat sat. **Dependent clause:** While it was raining, [followed by an independent clause] the cat sat.
Phrase: A group of words without a subject-verb component that is used as a single part of speech	Best friend With the yellow collar . . . For 600 nights. . . .
Noun Phrase: A phrase with a noun at its head	Those six leatherback turtles. . . .
Attributive Clause: A clause that classifies objects and is nonreversible; changing the order of the clause would change the meaning.	A square is a rectangle.
Identifying Clause: Clauses that define technical terms by creating a bridge to a less technical term.	Informational books are books that give facts about real life.
Nominalization: A verb or process that is changed into a noun	The destruction of the rainforest (destruct become destruction)

disciplinary subject matters) to more clearly convey information. Different registers incorporate different forms of syntax and rules of grammar; hence our emphasis is on how syntactic features of speech or texts are related to and used in different academic registers (mathematical registers, book reading registers). Some examples of features of complex syntax and important grammatical terms are provided in Table 1.2.

The order and inclusion of words plays a critical role in understanding, particularly in written text, where the writer must use language to convey meaning to the reader due to the distance between them. A conversation between two people may be supported by the context in which it takes place, but written text does not have this support for developing meaning. Instead, a writer must use language to provide the context. This precise language frequently requires complex syntax, or phrases and clauses that elaborate meaning through providing specific details. Not surprisingly, strong understanding of complex syntax is associated with improved reading comprehension (Mokhtari & Thompson, 2006; Nation & Snowling, 2000).

Discourse-Level Elements: Tone, Topic, Genre, and Contextualization

Moving up the levels of language, the discourse of academic registers emphasizes the tone and stance of the speaker (or text), as well as the degree of contextualization. We examine how discourse features are structured in a way that is typical of a particular social task. Linguistic choices are linked to the social purpose of the form of communication (written or oral). In other words, language choices reflect the purpose of communication (conveying information, making social connections) in a particular place (classrooms, homes, meetings) with particular participants (students, family, coworkers). How we talk changes based on these features, particularly in terms of tone and stance. Understanding the role of these features in oral or written communication can improve comprehension.

At the discourse level, the content or topic of talk may align more closely with a specific register, with academic registers typically focusing on the transmission of academic knowledge such as mathematics, science, language arts, and social studies. These academic topics would certainly be more challenging to a young student than familiar topics commonly found in home or casual registers (Westby, 1985) relating to the task at hand, interpersonal relationships, or current events.

An academic register relies on elements of decontextualized talk, which are used to discuss nonpresent topics that have occurred or will occur outside of the physical context. Decontextualized talk includes no presupposition of shared or existing knowledge between the interlocutors (participants), hence language (grammatical and lexical elements) is included to create clarity of understanding. Decontextualized language can be contrasted with contextualized language, which is talk about the here and now for which meaning is supported by the immediate surroundings and shared knowledge. Children begin using contextualized language prior to decontextualized language, hence decontextualized language may be viewed as a more sophisticated form of language use.

CONCLUSION

Academic language is the specialized language of the classroom that is used to convey academic content. It contains unique features at the word, sentence, and discourse levels that are shaped by the purpose and participants. Students arrive in classrooms with varying degrees of knowledge of academic language, all requiring some degree of support to become proficient. The following chapters provide in-depth descriptions of the features of academic language, along with strategies and activities for teaching from and with academic language.

CHAPTER 2

Language Learning

> **PRIMING QUESTIONS:**
> 1. What are the different components of language?
> 2. What aspects of language are children typically acquiring in the preschool to 3rd-grade years?
> 3. How do parents and teachers help children learn language?

Language is a remarkably complex and uniquely human capacity that children in all cultures learn in the first years of life. It is a capacity that is of pivotal importance to our lives. We use it to express love, to build friendships, to teach, to collaborate with others, to construct our personal life histories, and to preserve, recall, and celebrate our cultural histories.

What exactly is language and how do children learn it in what seems to be an effortless manner? In this chapter, we will skim the surface of a host of enormously complex issues as we briefly introduce you to language and language learning. Readers interested in deeper explanations and citations to original research about language and learning will find wonderful information in *Language Files: Materials for an Introduction to Language and Linguistics* (12th edition, Department of Linguistics, Ohio State University).

PRINCIPLES OF LANGUAGE LEARNING

Humans are uniquely equipped to learn language and are able to master phonological regularities, acquire basic syntax, learn words, and acquire mastery of basic conversational norms with limited intentional adult support.

Phonology

During the first year of life, babies begin experimenting with the sounds they can produce as they babble. All babies babble, even deaf infants; we are genetically programmed to begin producing sounds. We also are able to hear and distinguish different speech sounds. In fact, babies come to recognize their mothers' voices in utero and even the cadence and sound of books that they have heard being read aloud. Biology programs us to begin speaking and equips us to understand speech, but the environment shapes how we use these abilities. Children benefit from hearing sounds spoken clearly, and most acquire the ability to produce sounds accurately without special tutoring. By the end of the first year, the sounds that babies produce begin to reflect those of the language they are hearing. Throughout the preschool years, children progressively learn to produce sounds in the manner of their speech community. Children reared in bilingual or multilingual homes are advantaged in that they retain the ability to speak using the inflections and speech patterns of native speakers.

Words

As children acquire proficiency with detecting and manipulating the sounds in spoken language, they begin to develop an understanding of words. Harris et al. (2011) put forth the following principles for word learning:

- Frequency matters! Words that are encountered more frequently are more likely to be learned.
- Providing extended descriptions and definitions of words facilitates learning.
- Exposure to the word in multiple, supportive contexts allows students to experience how the word may be used in different grammatical and topical environments.
- Opportunities to use the word are critical. Children need many opportunities to use the word in a variety of contexts to build depth and breadth of understanding.
- Engagement with the word (mental manipulation) and discussions around spelling and the units of meaning in words, the morphological units, may aid in learning.

Estimates of the number of words that children learn vary, but there is general agreement that by 1st grade children know about 6,000 words. During the schooling years, they continue to learn about 2.5 root words per day, or roughly 900 a year (Biemiller & Slonim, 2001). However, these figures are a bit deceptive. Rather than fully mastering two or three words a day, children acquire partial knowledge of dozens of words a day. As they hear and read words multiple times and in different contexts, they slowly learn how to pronounce them (their phonology), how they are used in sentences (syntax), and the social contexts in which they are used (pragmatics).

While all children are adept at learning words, variability in exposure to varied words can result in enormous differences in the number of words that children understand and can use when they enter school. An added challenge is the variation in the extent to which the words that children learn in their home match those used and valued in school. Only some of the vocabulary that a child learns at home is relevant in classrooms.

Syntax

In order to communicate even basic wishes and ideas, we need to put words together into phrases and sentences. Each language has its own implicit rules, or regularities, that determine acceptable word order. These implicit rules, called the syntax or grammar of a language, are extremely subtle. Indeed, linguists have worked endlessly trying to describe the regularities that govern how we order words. Miraculously, children begin to master the basic syntactic patterns of their language in the preschool years. This occurs in a generally predictable pattern. For example, English-speaking children first learn simple active tense sentences that include only one clause and later master syntactic structures such as passives ("the car was hit by the truck") and relative clauses ("the man *with the blue hat*, is my father").

Humans are genetically equipped to learn to sequence words in ways that conform to the manner employed by their culture. There is great controversy regarding how this occurs, whether it reflects innate cognitive processing mechanisms or is the byproduct of how language is used. What is important for teachers is knowing that children are adept at acquiring and using the basic syntax of their language. However, just as for words, children need to hear and have opportunities to use less common and more advanced syntactic forms in order to master them. Similarly, there is variability in how quickly children master advanced syntactic forms such as passives and relative clauses and the more advanced syntax found in academic language. This variability is related to opportunities to hear and use language.

Discourse

We assemble sentences into sequences of language called discourse and use that language in a manner appropriate to the social context. Linguists use the term *pragmatics* to refer to knowledge of how and when to use language in a particular manner. In this text, we focus on academic language, which includes a complex assemblage of knowledge about language and how it is used. Discourse is structured by a host of implicit rules specific to different communities of language users. For example, children learn conversational patterns such as how to respond to questions with particular kinds of information (e.g., "What do you want to eat?" "A cookie!"). These patterns of discourse carry social meanings. As they learn to converse, children learn to show respect to elders by using specific terms (e.g., *sir* or *ma'am* in certain cultures), by modulating how much, how loudly, and what they say and how to position their body when replying (e.g., look the speaker in the eye or avoid eye contact; stand erect and display confidence or look down and appear meek and compliant). Children also acquire verbal skill with forms of discourse as they talk with peers, for example as they learn to tell jokes, tease, and even tell lies. These communicative patterns are acquired gradually, and children gain skill as they practice using them.

The ability to understand and effectively use genres is an endlessly challenging task that students and adults never cease struggling to master. It is very helpful to be skilled in using many different forms of discourse, because one demonstrates competence in an endeavor by how one participates in conversations. Discourse ability draws upon one's facility using syntax and vocabulary. Children who can use varied syntactic structures and have large vocabularies are in a position to use and understand increasingly complex forms of discourse. Those with less advanced language skills need added support.

FACILITATING LANGUAGE

Although adults may not intentionally seek to teach language structures, careful study of parent–child interactions has revealed that certain ways of engaging with children enhance the speed of learning (Golinkoff et al., 2015). Research that examines the effectiveness of instruction designed to teach language has built on that observational research and enriched our understanding of how adults can intentionally support language in classrooms. Teachers who understand which conversational techniques foster learning can be more intentional about adopting effective methods. We call these *language learning principles*. These are tips you can adapt and employ throughout the day and as you plan your instruction.

Expose Students to Many, Varied Language Features

In order to learn language structures (word pronunciation, vocabulary, syntax, discourse genres) and ways of using language (pragmatics), we must hear them. This may seem obvious, but it is of critical importance. In everyday interactions, adults typically do not intentionally teach language, but children still acquire skill using it. Children learn words and ways of using language because they hear the vocabulary and syntactic structures used many times. Think back to when you were trying to learn a new language. Whether you were learning in a classroom or while participating in a culture where the language was being spoken, you needed to hear the words and grammatical structures used many times in order to master them.

Exposure has two dimensions: *quantity* and *variety*. *Quantity* of exposure matters: We more quickly learn words, syntactic forms, and discourse forms that we hear more often (Huttenlocher et al., 2002). The *variety* of words and structures that we hear is also critical. Up until 3 years old, sheer quantity is especially important, but in the preschool and early schooling years, the quality of exposure becomes most important (Rowe, 2012).

Teachers play a critical role in exposing children to many different words and structures that children typically do not hear in everyday life. New instructional topics naturally provide occasions to use new vocabulary. Consider a unit of study of the local community, a common topic in early childhood classrooms. Books, videos, a classroom visitor, or a trip to the firehouse could lead to use of a host of novel words and phrases (e.g., "water pressure, extension ladder, paramedic, evacuation.)" An activity like a scientific investigation can lead to talk about hypotheses and observations that use complex syntactic frames. For example, students might talk about their mental states: "I believe, I thought, I noticed, I wondered." These mental state verbs are followed by relative clauses, ". . . that the boat would sink." Thus, the nature of the activity scaffolds students' ability to use more advanced syntactic forms.

Quantity and variety are two powerful levers for teaching language. In order to make them work for your students, you must be *intentional*. Select books with an eye toward the complexity and appeal of the language, plan units of instruction that are intellectually stimulating and will enable you to introduce new concepts and vocabulary, and engage in conversations that deal with interesting topics that will naturally involve use of varied words. When you choose a book to read, and plan units and instructional activities, select key words and concepts that you will teach. If you take the time to select key words, you will become more attuned to the variety of words that you are teaching, will be more intentional about using those words, and will be more alert to occasions when children use them. You will gain word awareness and, with your help, children can become more aware of the words and language forms they are learning.

Help Students Use Language

It is not enough to hear words and sentences. For mastery, students need to be involved in interactions that give them a meaningful reason to use them. The amount of time that students talk helps predict how many words they will learn from instruction. However, children do not get to use language very often in classrooms. One study that recorded audio of preschoolers throughout a day found that, on average, a 3- or 4-year-old child tended to be silent over half the day (Dickinson & Tabors, 2001). In kindergarten and primary-grade classrooms, it is also difficult to structure activities in ways that ensure students are regularly using language.

One way to increase how often students use language is to provide time for them to engage in activities of their own choosing with peers. Pretend play and block building are wonderful settings for talk in preschool and kindergarten classrooms. In primary-grade classrooms, teachers can create projects or provide games that foster language use. Beneficial as these peer interactions are, the most educationally enriching conversational opportunities are those when students talk with a teacher one-on-one or in a small group. One study found conversations that preschool teachers had with students during their choice time were related to those students' end-of-kindergarten vocabulary (Dickinson & Porche, 2011). That vocabulary, in turn, helped predict 4th-grade reading. Importantly, it was not the number of conversations, but the quality that mattered. Those in which students played an important role were best—students learned more when they talked more.

In order to ensure that your students get to use language, you need to be *intentional*: Plan activities when students must talk. This book suggests many such activities. You also need to take advantage of all opportunities for informal conversations with individuals or small groups. Transition times, times when students are working on self-directed activities, meals, and snacks are examples of occasions when you may be able to engage children in conversations. As you have such personalized conversations, you also build a deeper emotional bond with the student, learning important information about their interests, fears, out-of-school activities, and families.

Engage in Responsive, Individualized, and Sustained Conversations

Three aspects of adult–child conversations support learning to the extent that adults are responsive to the student's interest, tailor their responses to the needs of the student, and sustain the conversation. Each of these elements have been studied separately, but a skilled teacher will weave them together in a tapestry of support for students during a conversation. For example, consider this conversation that occurred between Cindy, a preschool teacher, and her students when they were exploring a pond. Andy, a student, was interested in a lily pad that was next to the pond and asked where it came from. Picking up on this question, Cindy engaged him and others in an extended discussion. First, she is responsive to Andy's interest and asks yes/no questions to draw him into a conversation.

> Cindy: Oh, you think this came from the tree and somehow ended up in the water? Or do you think it grows in the water? *[Andy points to the lily pad lying on the ground next to the pond in response. Cindy then puts into words what she believes to be Andy's intention in pointing.]*
> Cindy: It grew up from the water over there? (points)
> Andy: Yeah. *[She sustains the conversation by using an open-ended question.]*
> Cindy: What do you think about this long, long stem? *[Andy pauses while having trouble formulating an answer to this hard question. So, Cindy decides to provide more information and possibly put into words a complex idea that Andy is having.]*

Cindy: It grows with it. *[She then asks another open-ended question to encourage clarification.]*

Cindy: It grows with the lily pad? *[Christina, who is an English language learner, was watching and now joins the conversation. She uses the word "frog" as she stumbles trying to express her idea while jumping.]*

Christina: No because the. . . . *[Cindy listens carefully, intuits the child's meaning, and puts it into a clear statement.]*

Cindy: Oh, you think that if you don't have this part, this stem, the frog can't jump. It can't jump off the lily pad?

Christina: Yeah.

What started as a one-on-one conversation became a small-group discussion. Note elements of this wonderful chance, but intentional conversation. The teacher *noticed* what children were interested in; rather than providing a simple answer, she drew them into a thought-provoking conversation as she sought to understand their thinking while helping them formulate and express hypotheses. She used a yes/no question to invite engagement and an open-ended question that probed for deeper thinking. She *listened* carefully and *revoiced* the students' ideas, building on and shaping their words and ideas into well-formulated sentences. Note, in particular, the *extended* nature of the interaction. This transcript is only the first half of this wonderful exploration of the lily pad. Each of these strategies is critically important to having such a conversation:

- *Noticing and listening:* Teachers need to observe and notice what children are interested in and understand how they are thinking about things in order to engage in conversations that make the most of teachable moments.
- *Revoicing:* When teachers reframe students' statement or put their ideas into words, they model how skilled language users talk about the object or phenomenon. They supply the precise vocabulary and appropriate sentence structure for encoding that idea.
- *Sustained interaction:* By listening to students and probing their thinking, the teacher engaged in a sustained interaction. Sustained conversations, when they occur in children's homes, have been found to be associated with brain growth (Romeo, Leonard et al., 2018; Romeo, Segaran et al., 2018) and have been found to support learning in classrooms as well. Teachers have difficulty finding time to engage in extended interactions. We suggest that you "strive for five" back and forth exchanges (Teacher-Student-Teacher-Student-Teacher, or vice-versa). If you achieve five exchanges, you will have reached well beyond the typical length of a classroom conversation.

Teachers who are responsive to students' interests, who listen carefully, revoice their ideas, and sustain conversations over multiple turns, are individualizing instruction. Such conversations, tailored to the needs and interests of students, are ideal vehicles for building children's language abilities.

CONCLUSION

Children's ability to learn language is a complex and miraculous accomplishment. Between birth and 3rd grade, children acquire skill using many elements of their community's language system; they build relationship, express needs, and learn about the world. Children are biologically prepared to acquire language, but teachers are entrusted with the role of fostering this learning, especially with helping students learn the sophisticated and challenging elements of language that comprise academic language. Intentionality is key to a teachers' success in this endeavor. As you plan, teach lessons, and have chance informal conversations, strive to expose children to varied language structures and engage them in sustained conversations that encourage them to use language in ways that stretch their language competencies.

CHAPTER 3

Linguistic Diversity and Registers

PRIMING QUESTIONS:

1. What is a register?
2. What are some distinctions between academic registers and more casual registers?
3. How might you sustain the diverse linguistic assets that your students bring to school while simultaneously growing all students' competence with academic language?

THE ACADEMIC REGISTER

Academic register is a broad term for the patterns of talk commonly used in classroom settings. Registers are patterns of language content and form used in different social contexts. A register includes the vocabulary and grammatical features of speech in a particular context, but also the social or pragmatic uses of language, including conversational norms and nonverbal communication. Word-, sentence-, and discourse-level features may change based on the participants, place, and purpose of the interaction. Registers typically feature unspoken rules that are part of an understanding by members of a group participating in an event. Thus, registers vary based on the content, the people, and the function of the language in context (Halliday, 1978; Schleppegrell, 2001).

We encounter various registers in all aspects of our life, and these registers evolve to fit the purpose of the people and context. For example, sportscasters use particular features of language—vocabulary, syntax, intonation—uncommonly used in other settings. When two sportscasters are engaging in play-by-play reporting and color commentary, they follow particular discourse patterns together and their style, cadence, word choice, and grammar match their role. You may hear an ESPN announcer using sentence fragments, slang, and technical sports jargon. While these types of language use may not be common for academic purposes, no one questions the appropriateness for the sportscasting field. A very different register is employed by actors performing Shakespeare or adopting Shakespearean style for another performance. The metaphorical language, playful rhythm of iambic pentameter, and Elizabethan vocabulary comprise a period-specific and recognizable register of its own. This register may be rarely used on street corners or in early childhood classrooms, although it may be heard in high school English classrooms or among theater troupes.

Both children and adults may employ a wide array of registers in different contexts. A range of specific "home" and "school" registers are employed in various settings throughout the United States. Similarly, many other social places in the community have their own unique registers. An adult may use different ways of speaking at home, work, with friends, or at the grocery store. Similarly, children may vary their registers at home and in the classroom, but also on the basketball court, at recess, and in church. All of these registers have unique rules and linguistic features.

Children can learn to shift from one register to another in different contexts, but often need adult support as they acquire these skills. Take 6-year-old Brayden, who is developing skill at using various registers depending on social context. In casual situations with peers, Brayden confidently uses language to play and communicate.

"Whatcha playin'?" Before school starts, Brayden spends the morning in the schoolyard, laughing and playing with his friends. He joins in with some friends reciting double-dutch rhymes. "Strawberry shortcake, cream on top . . ." When the bell rings, he grabs his backpack and heads inside, commenting to his friend Miles on the way, "Like your shoes. Those are sweet!" When he reaches his 1st-grade classroom, Brayden smiles when his teacher greets him at the door. "Good morning, Ms. Thomas!"

The academic register is generally characterized by more formal language, including precise vocabulary, complex syntax, structured discourse norms, and content-focused concepts (Schleppegrell, 2012). In academic settings, this type of language is used to communicate arguments and complex and abstract ideas. In contrast, nonacademic registers typically feature more casual language that includes slang or jargon, informal use of grammar, relaxed conversational norms, and content focused on the concrete, immediate context (van Kleeck, 2014). Table 3.1 includes real-world examples of young children engaging in both the academic register and more casual registers typical of home and community settings. One thing that you will notice is that the teacher plays a key role in modeling, facilitating, and structuring opportunities in the classroom to encourage students' use of the academic register.

Some children experience the academic register prior to starting school if their caregivers adopt a school-like register when reading bedtime stories, shopping at the grocery store, having dinner table conversations that include talk about past or future experiences, or doing activities like cooking

Table 3.1. Examples of Features of Academic Registers and Casual Registers

ACADEMIC REGISTER	CASUAL REGISTER
Vocabulary	
[Leila in the prekindergarten classroom block center]	[Leila playing with LEGO™ at home with a sibling]
Teacher: What part of our community are you going to build today?	*Leila:* I'm hungry.
Leila: I'm going to build the community center.	*Michael:* Me, too. (*pauses*) Can you hand me that one?
Jackson: Can I help you?	*Leila:* Which one?
Leila: Sure. You can work on the driveway and parking lot. You'll need some of these long, skinny blocks.	*Michael:* The big blue one.
	Leila: Here. Whatcha making?
Teacher: What else does the community center need?	*Michael:* Argos's tower. From the movie.
	Leila: Whoa! I'm going to make one too.
Leila: Ours has two buildings. One for families and one for older people.	*Father:* Nice tower, Michael. Time for lunch!
Teacher: Ah, senior citizens. That's the Senior Center. So, two structures?	
Syntax	
[Terrence listening to his kindergarten teacher read a book aloud]	[Terrence sharing a book with a friend on the bus]
Terrence: What is that?	*Terrence:* Look at this one!
Teacher: Oh, here you can see where Amelia is discovering the secret door. Where do you think it leads?	*Miles:* Lemme see. (*pauses)* Oooh. Can you lift the flap?
Terrence: I think it leads into another world.	*Terrence:* Yeah. It's a dragon!
	Miles: And an egg!
Teacher: What makes you think that, Terrence?	*Terrence:* Yep.
	Miles: Are there anymore?
Terrence: On the last page, Amelia was talking about looking for another world.	*Terrence:* Right here. Another egg. That's three.
Gaby: I don't think so. There is no such thing as a door to another world.	

Discourse	
[Lola in a small-group science exploration in her 2nd-grade classroom] *Lola:* So, we're supposed to predict which things will be attracted to the magnet and which ones won't. *Marianne:* The paperclip will, because it's made out of metal. *Lola:* Yeah, I think so too. I also think this nail will stick to the magnet. But the pebble won't. *Theo:* And the pencil won't either. It's not made of metal. I'm not sure about the key. What do y'all think? *Marianne:* You're right about the pencil. . . . I think the key will stick. It is made out of metal. *Lola:* Okay, we've made our predictions. Now let's test them out.	[Lola at recess with friends] *Sasha:* Come here, Lola! *Lola:* What are y'all doin'? *Elliott:* Looking for four-leaf clovers. *Sasha:* They're good luck. *Lola:* Okay. I'll help. Here's one! *Elliott:* No, it's not. *Lola:* Oh, right. Okay, I'll keep looking. *Sasha:* I don't think there are any. *Elliott:* Keep looking! There's gotta be some. *Lola:* I never find any. But I'll look. *Sasha:* Three . . . three . . . three. *Lola:* None over here. All three-leaf clovers. *Elliott:* Found one!

or woodworking together. Other children may first encounter the academic register when they start formal education in pre-K or kindergarten and therefore need more time and teaching to adopt the features of the academic register. For example, a prekindergarten student may be confused when a teacher first asks them a known-answer question such as, "What color is this block?" if the child was not previously asked these "test-like" questions at home. The degree of similarity between the registers that a child is familiar with outside of school and the academic register has been shown to predict how the child is perceived by their teachers and their academic outcomes (Delpit & Dowdy, 2008; Souto-Manning, 2013). Thus, the academic register becomes part of the "hidden curriculum" of schooling that warrants your thoughtful consideration and your support of students as they acquire command of this register.

While academic register is a broad term for language use in classrooms, in fact many more specific registers may be used within and between early childhood classroom settings. For example, as shown in Table 3.1, the language used in a block center in pre-K will differ in form, content, and formality from the language used during a read-aloud in a kindergarten classroom and from a hands-on science lesson in 2nd grade. Each context features unique language use. In your classroom, you can call attention to the unique features of specific classroom registers by naming them and modeling their features. How do we talk like a scientist? What are our math talk moves? What's the best way to share feedback on a classmate's writing? Lead your students in noticing and adopting the academic register used in early childhood classrooms.

Halfway through his kindergarten year, Brayden has already adopted some of the rules and norms of academic register usage for specific content and purposes in the classroom while maintaining other registers for less formal interactions.

> Brayden's class starts the day with a literacy block. In small group reading instruction, he volunteers a complex sentence about the book they are preparing to read, "I predict it is going to be about astronauts, because I see that planet and the spaceship on the cover." This statement mirrors similar predictions that his teacher has modeled and asked students to make throughout the school year. Later, while sitting with a friend in the classroom library, Brayden switches to more casual language, "Hey, look at this!" and giggles while he points to another book's cover. During a math lesson later in the day, Brayden works with a group of peers to identify two- and three-dimensional shapes. "This one is definitely a sphere," he states with confidence as he holds up a small globe.

The academic register features "literate" language prominently and typically privileges academic language over more casual language. However, early childhood classrooms are diverse places, and students bring many linguistic assets to the classroom to make it a rich place for speaking and listening, reading and writing. Young children are already adept at navigating the use of different social language practices across different contexts. For example, when they are in formal settings such as a library, they know that there are norms for talking (and not talking), asking questions, and addressing adults that are different from at home. While school registers featuring academic language have traditionally been valued, all children come to school with command of multiple registers and related "funds of knowledge" of language use for a variety of purposes (González et al., 2006). Thus, while learning and using academic language is essential in school settings, the academic register in early childhood classrooms must build on the diverse quilt of home and community linguistic capital that students bring to the school context.

You play an important role in fostering students' linguistic awareness of the academic register and building their facility with using academic talk for a variety of purposes. This requires explicit instruction in aspects of academic language and setting up a classroom environment and activities that provide occasions to use academic talk and build metalinguistic awareness. At the same time, your students are likely to bring experience with a wide range of other registers, as well as variations on English or multilingual capabilities. This linguistic diversity is tied to all other areas of students' identity: family, community, race or ethnicity, religion, geography, and history. You should consider this linguistic diversity in your academic language instruction to simultaneously apprentice students into the academic register *and* affirm the linguistic assets that all of your students bring.

TEACHING LINGUISTICALLY DIVERSE STUDENTS

Today's early childhood classrooms are increasingly diverse, and you may find that your students have a variety of backgrounds and experiences with language. This diversity signals that you need to explicitly make teaching the academic register and building all students' awareness about linguistic diversity the rule rather than the exception (Lobeck, 2019). This approach is inclusive, because all young children are learning the language of schooling during the pre-K through 3rd-grade years.

Multilingualism

One aspect of linguistic diversity in today's classrooms is multilingualism. As of 2017, more than 10% of U.S. public school students were identified as English language learners (ELLs) (Hussar et al., 2020), and that percentage is growing each year. Beyond these students, you may have students who are not identified as ELLs but hear and speak other languages at home or in their communities. While students who are multilingual may need a variety of supports as they learn a new language, there are many assets to being multilingual. Bilingualism or multilingualism is associated with greater cognitive functions and metalinguistic awareness.

Cummins (1979, 1981) drew a distinction between the interpersonal and academic language that multilingual learners acquire as they learn English. English learners typically acquire a strong command of Basic Interpersonal Communication Skills (BICS) first, which are the linguistic skills used for the casual, social talk characteristic of out-of-school registers. BICS is mastered by the intermediate fluency stage of second language acquisition, but Cognitive Academic Language Proficiency (CALP) takes longer to master. CALP requires the use of the formal, abstract linguistic skills characteristic of the academic register, including specialized vocabulary and complex grammar. You may have multilingual students in your classroom who appear fluent in English due to a strong command of BICS. Yet those students are likely still developing CALP, as they are simultaneously learning English as an additional language and the academic register.

At school, you can help multilingual students add to their BICS by explicitly teaching and providing scaffolds for academic language.

Evidence-based scaffolds and teaching strategies for English learners are covered at length in other resources and include frequent opportunities for peer interaction, use of visuals and nonverbal cues to accompany language, and building upon students' background knowledge. At the same time, you should ensure that students' home languages are valued in the classroom (Souto-Manning, 2016). Provide multilingual children and their families the opportunity to share their language capital with the class through teaching peers new words, sharing books and music, and explaining differences in the languages that they know. Students who are multilingual may be encouraged to "code-switch" between their native language and English at appropriate times, such as in peer collaborations in centers, conversations at lunch or snack times, or in oral storytelling or writing. Teachers can encourage children to employ their first language to help them understand and then better communicate in English. Such movement between languages is called translanguaging, and has been found to be an effective way to support reading comprehension (Garcia & Kleifgen, 2020). Another important consideration is working with families to ensure the native language is maintained in both oral language and literacy at home to support the academic register in multiple languages.

Language Variation

An additional feature of linguistic diversity is dialect. Dialect is a pattern of language variation (Adger et al., 2014; Reaser et al., 2017). Much like a native language, dialect is a feature of one's identity and may be shaped by an individual's geographical region, age, race or ethnicity, socioeconomic status, gender, and other characteristics. Thus, while some dialectical features may be more prominent in certain settings, an individual's dialect remains present at all times. At home or in casual settings with friends, children may employ all of the features of their dialect. At school, while using an academic register, children may use fewer features of their dialect. However, certain dialectal features such as accent and vocabulary will likely still be present in the classroom.

You can capitalize on the linguistic diversity of your students by affirming students' home language and dialect. As you support your students' academic language development, it is important to also provide opportunities for students to use their own language and dialect in the classroom whether while conversing with peers or in creative activities such as writing and performing. Code-switching between dialects in spoken language may be encouraged for students with dialectal diversity just as with multilingual students (Reaser et al., 2017). In this way, teachers can also explicitly celebrate students' diverse language, dialect, and command of various registers.

You can build your students' linguistic awareness by explicitly teaching about classroom language use and the academic register (Reaser et al.,

Figure 3.1. Anchor Chart Highlighting Features of Academic Registers and Casual Registers

Formal Language	Informal Language
When to use: • At school or work • With people we don't know well	When to use: • With friends and family • While playing • In texts or chats
• "Hello. How are you?" • "You are welcome." • "Let's begin with page 12." • "Mr.Williams just arrived." • "Would you like to join our group?"	• "Hi! What's up?" • "No problem!" • "Let's do it." • "You're my BFF." • "Come over here!" • "Wanna chip?"

2017). You may highlight various aspects of *academic talk* and *casual talk* in a way that affirms both as appropriate for different settings. These discussions also provide a launching point for teaching academic vocabulary, syntax, and discourse for the classroom throughout the year. Some teachers conceptualize this as formal and informal language, particularly for writing (see Figure 3.1).

CELEBRATING LINGUISTIC DIVERSITY WHILE FOSTERING ACADEMIC LANGUAGE DEVELOPMENT

Many classroom settings provide opportunities for teachers to foster academic language learning while simultaneously affirming students' linguistic diversity. Three prime activities for highlighting use of different registers and building metalinguistic awareness include book reading, sharing time, and writing instruction.

Book Reading

Teachers can use children's literature in culturally-affirming lessons about differences between school and nonschool registers and code-switching. Most books, including children's picture books, feature academic language that reflect the school register. These books provide students exposure to academic language, and students need knowledge of academic language to comprehend these texts. However, early childhood classrooms need to include an inclusive collection of books representing characters and voices from people of all races/ethnicities, languages, religions, regions, and abilities. This diverse collection for reading aloud, instruction, listening centers, and children's own reading should also include books that represent linguistic diversity and a variety of registers. Multilingual texts highlight connections and beautiful differences between English and other languages and validate code-switching as a literate practice. Dual-language picture books that will capture young children's attention are listed in Table 3.2 and Appendix D. One challenge may be your comfort with reading or the ability to pronounce the language or dialect. Consider using audiobooks or video recordings of the author reading, or inviting in family or community members to share these texts or others of their choice reflecting their home

Table 3.2. Children's Literature Featuring Language Variation and Multilingualism

Title	Author (Year)	Language Diversity Featured
Don't Say Ain't	Smalls (2004)	African American dialect
I am Every Good Thing	Barnes (2020)	African American dialect
When I Was Young in the Mountains	Rylant (1993)	Appalachian dialect
The Swirling Hijaab	Robert (2002)	Arabic bilingual
The Cloud Artist	Maret (2017)	Choctaw bilingual
Dragonfly Kites	Highway (2016)	Cree bilingual
The King Cake Baby	Dawson (2015)	French Creole dialect
Priya Dreams of Marigolds and Masala	Patel (2019)	Indian bilingual
Chinese New Year Wishes	Lin (2019)	Mandarin Chinese bilingual
Friends from the Other Side/Amigos del otro lado	Anzaldua (1997)	Spanish bilingual
La Princesa and the Pea	Elya (2017)	Spanish bilingual
Juana and Lucas	Medina (2019)	Spanish bilingual
Niño Wrestles the World	Morales (2015)	Spanish bilingual
Islandborn	Díaz (2018)	Spanish bilingual/ Caribbean dialect
Jalapeño Bagels	Wing (1996)	Spanish and Yiddish multilingual
Chicken Sunday	Polacco (1998)	Multiple dialects
Your Name Is a Song	Thompkins-Bigelow (2020)	Names from various languages/cultures

language or dialect. You may use these books to highlight linguistic diversity, features of academic registers and other informal registers, and build a more inclusive classroom.

Sharing Time

Sharing time has been well-established as having its own register in classrooms. Many teachers implement "show and tell" or sharing as part of a morning meeting. Students take turns sharing artifacts or stories from outside of school with the class. This activity traditionally has its own language features and expectations that can sometimes exclude students whose experiences or narrative practices differ from that of the teacher or peers (Méndez Barletta, 2008; Michaels, 1981). You can create a more inclusive sharing time by establishing norms and expectations that build a safe community, while also explicitly encouraging students to share using their own dialect, home language, or code-switching practices as well as storytelling style (Gallagher, 2016). You can focus on clarifying meaning and model asking questions for clarity to help the sharer and their peers develop features of an academic narrative common in the school register. Some teachers do not have children bring new toys to share, partly because they can highlight economic disparities and because having the toy may limit the complexity of the child's contribution. A child may simply feel that showing the toy conveys the critical information. One other strategy is to limit how many children talk each day. This allows teachers and students to ask follow-up questions that prompt clarification. Also, when children know that they will be sharing, some parents help them think about what they can say.

Writing

Engaging young children in authentic writing experiences not only helps develop their early literacy practices and knowledge of academic discourses, but can also simultaneously affirm students' linguistic diversity and support students' code-switching between the academic register and casual registers (Dyson & Smitherman, 2009). All children can experiment with using their own voice in writing, particularly when writing narratives for purposes of telling or entertaining. Personal, realistic, or fictional narratives may feature dialogue from people or characters using a variety of registers depending on the setting. Having students create their own comics or graphic novels highlights the use of dialogue and oral language and can encourage having characters use different languages or dialects or switch registers in various scenes. Other modes of composition, such as informative or opinion writing, more typically feature academic language. Teaching the vocabulary, syntax, and discourse structure of those written genres calls attention to features of the academic register (Fogel & Ehri, 2000). There are a variety of

authentic writing tasks, including writing recipes or other procedural directions, and writing poetry or songs that lend themselves to this teaching. You
can support students' awareness of the structure of academic texts by making distinctions between the academic register and other familiar registers
while engaging with different texts. For example, students may be invited
to read and then write poems using a dialect of African American language
(Hartman & Machado, 2019) or compose bilingual poetry (Machado &
Hartman, 2019). Students who are multilingual should be encouraged to
write bilingual texts that include words, phrases, or sentences that would
be spoken at home or in their community or to educate others on their
language and culture. Not only do these practices affirm linguistic diversity
and build metalinguistic awareness, but they foster an inclusive classroom
community that celebrates many ways of using language.

A variety of digital tools can support listening to and speaking in the
academic register while also valuing various registers, home languages, and
dialects (Rowsell et al., 2016). Applications for digital storytelling, such as
Seesaw and VoiceThread, allow students to write, draw, and record artifacts
from their work. Students may listen to ebooks read in an academic register,
then use that language as a model to record a retelling in their own words.
Emergent writers can narrate a drawing or image using their own language
or dialect. Older students may respond to prompts related to any content
area, using sentence frames for structured practice with complex syntax in
an academic register. Using simple recording devices, including memo features on smartphones, children and their caregivers can record oral family
stories to share in listening centers.

All of these strategies support an inclusive and culturally affirming classroom, while also providing an entree into explicit instruction about academic
language. You will find a number of tools in this book to help you model, explicitly teach, and structure your classroom to support your students' acquisition of the academic register. At the same time, you can sustain students'
identities by validating their use of other registers, dialects, and languages in
and out of the classroom. Brayden's teacher calls attention to features of the
academic register, while also providing guidance for ways that Brayden can
incorporate familiar, casual registers into the classroom context.

> Ms. Thomas, Brayden's teacher, is talking with Brayden one-on-one about his
> writing project. He has been working on a personal narrative for several days,
> and he is really excited to show it to her. "I've got a beginning, middle, and
> end, and now I'm working on the illustrations," Brayden explains. Ms. Thomas
> complements his use of story structure and word choice. "Brayden, I see you
> added a lot of detail to your narrative. You even used the word 'sphere' when
> describing your new soccer ball." Then she adds, "But my favorite part may be
> your use of dialogue here. You can really hear your voice in the way you are
> shouting and celebrating with your teammates. It brings the story to life!"

CONCLUSION

Your knowledge of the features of various registers will allow you to support your young students in developing competence with the academic register. An early childhood teacher's role is to model, explicitly teach, and design opportunities for using the academic register in the classroom. Meanwhile, purposeful attention to students' linguistic diversity, including acknowledging and valuing the various registers that each student already knows, will enhance your powerful, inclusive teaching practices to build all students' linguistic awareness.

CHAPTER 4

Academic Vocabulary

> **PRIMING QUESTIONS:**
> 1. How do you choose the vocabulary terms that you teach?
> 2. Do you consider how difficult or easy the words are to learn when planning instruction?
> 3. What routines and materials do you incorporate?

The CCSS define academic vocabulary as "words that appear in a variety of content areas and have different meanings in different academic contexts" (Conley, 2014, p. 9). Simply put, academic vocabulary is the corpus of words used to engage with academic topics in classroom settings. Notice how this description of academic vocabulary specifies´use in content areas (classroom settings), which may vary dramatically across grade levels. For example, prekindergarten classrooms may have dramatic play centers, water/sand tables, circle time, and morning meeting as spaces for learning, with each having vocabulary associated with it. The academic vocabulary encountered in these settings may differ significantly from the academic vocabulary encountered in a 2nd-grade classroom. Therefore, it is essential to remember that academic vocabulary varies across academic spaces/disciplines and grade levels. Instruction and word selection may therefore be quite different across grade level and instructional activities.

There are two broad categories of academic vocabulary words. Nonspecialized academic words are those that may be found across academic content areas and have consistent definitions that do not change based on the academic discipline. Many of these terms are verbs that are useful for both reading and writing tasks. Given the general nature of these terms, they may be taught across a variety of disciplines and across the school year (in contrast to within a specific unit of study). As these terms tend to not have synonyms that can be used for quick instruction and word-to-concept mapping, we recommend teaching these high-utility words through engaging activities where students are enacting the term. For example, when learning the term *predict*, students should be making predictions during read-alouds or science experiments.

Nonspecialized Academic Vocabulary Terms

Term	Definition
Analyze	Break a problem or data set down into pieces
Compare	Tell how two or more things are similar, or what they have in common
Contrast	Tell how two or more things are different
Evaluate	Judge or determine the quality (good or bad, right or wrong) of a proposed solution
Explain	Tell how or why
Formulate	Come up with or develop a plan
Infer	Make a reasonable guess based on knowledge or data
Investigate	Explore a problem to find a solution or answer a question
Predict	Make a reasonable guess about what will happen in the future
Summarize	Tell the main ideas in a short statement
Support	Provide reasons or back up a claim

In contrast, specialized academic vocabulary are terms that have meanings specific to a discipline or that are associated primarily with a specific discipline. Words such as *measure* and *conduct* are specialized academic vocabulary terms as they may have different meanings based on the academic content. Consider how these terms would have different meanings in music (a *measure* of written music and *conducting* a symphony) and science class (*measuring* quantities and *conducting* energy). Other terms such as *filibuster*, *biodiversity*, and *hypotenuse* are specialized academic vocabulary terms associated with specific academic disciplines. These terms are rarely, if ever, used outside of their disciplines and have definitions that are consistent regardless of the context. Instruction of these specialized academic vocabulary terms should occur within the related discipline.

In this chapter, we discuss methods for selecting and teaching academic vocabulary. Consideration for levels of difficulty of the terms are provided, as well as instructional routines and materials. This chapter focuses on general methods for academic vocabulary selection and instruction across academic domains. More specific guidance for discipline-specific academic vocabulary instruction can be found in later chapters.

SELECTING WORDS TO TEACH

Decades of research have yet to identify which words should be taught at which points in time. However, there are a few common threads that are agreed upon:

1. Teach words that students do not yet know. While this may seem simple, it is a bit more complex. Teachers may select words such as *tree* or *sun* as target vocabulary words, arguing that they will teach about the scientific features of each that the students do not yet know. Students already know and use these words, but they may not yet have depth and breadth of understanding. If you want to teach for breadth and depth, then teach associated terms. For example, if you want to increase understanding of *trees*, consider less well-known words such as *bark, oxygen, phloem, xylem, trunk*, and *photosynthesis*. Spending time on known words reduces instructional time for novel words.
2. Teach words that are useful. Utility involves being able to understand the words in texts and/or use them in conversation or writing. Often, words are chosen that relate to a current topic of study. Utility is dependent on the context, so consider how, when, and where students might use these words and how important they are for understanding new content. Also, consider how the words might relate to the child's life and how the words appear in the materials and texts in your classroom.
3. Teach words that are conceptually related. Teaching words in conceptually related clusters provides critical information about the meanings, uses, or purposes. For example, indicating that a strawberry is a fruit gives clues that a strawberry is a food, is something that grows on a plant, and contains at least one seed. A child who understands these properties of fruits may develop a stronger understanding of a novel fruit. For example, by telling a child that a tangelo is a fruit, the child who understands the properties of a fruit can extend these to the tangelo. Categorization may serve as a bootstrap for learning new words (Neuman et al., 2011). Building conceptual knowledge may assist with building vocabulary depth and breadth.

These three guidelines are useful for selecting useful terms, but more is needed to determine the amount of instructional time that each term deserves. More challenging words require more instruction. Consider the principles for word learning discussed in Chapter 2, as these are helpful for considering the degree of challenge for each word. We know that students tend to learn the words they hear the most frequently. Academic vocabulary words tend to appear less frequently in casual conversation; hence students may require more support to acquire these terms. While we cannot accurately gauge how often a specific student has heard a particular word, we do have some general ideas about how frequently certain words appear in the world around us. There are lists specifically devoted to academic vocabulary that may be electronically searched. Two commonly used word lists are Coxhead's Academic Word List (AWL) and the Gardner and Davies Academic Vocabulary List. These lists categorize academic vocabulary according to the amount of usage in language (not academic texts), noting which words appear the most frequently. The Words and Phrases tool (www.wordandphrase.info) is an easy and free tool that will highlight academic vocabulary in digital text and categorize them based on their frequency. These lists do not categorize terms based on grade levels. Consider selecting academic terms that appear frequently, as these are terms that students will likely need to know to read and produce academic texts and discussions.

Core Vocabulary

Hiebert et al. (2018) developed a set of core vocabulary terms that account for a large percentage of words found in school texts. As these terms are found in school texts, they are considered academic vocabulary. This list contains 2,500-word families that constitute 97% of the words found in the exemplar K–1 complex texts as named within the Next Generation Science Standards (NGSS). This list divides words up into conceptually related clusters (e.g., emotions, animals) for instructional purposes. Many of these terms have multiple meanings that may depend upon the context in which the word is used. Approximately 32% of the terms on this list are concrete (see next subsection). These high-utility words are worthy of instruction.

Concreteness and Imageability

Other factors can also be considered for determining the degree of difficulty for matching with appropriate instruction, such as the degree of concreteness or imageability (Brysbaert et al., 2014; Maguire et al., 2006). Both imageability and concreteness refer to the level of abstraction of the vocabulary term. Highly abstract words may be processes (mental or physical), or very large or small in scope (galaxy versus microcosm), making them challenging to conceptualize or visualize. Highly concrete words tend to have a more regular physical shape and are tangible. For example, *cup* is more concrete than *evaporate*, as *cup* is easier to represent visually than *evaporate*. The degree of concreteness can also be determined through an examination of the definition of the term. Highly concrete terms tend to include a physical description in their definition. Again, consider the words *cup* (a small bowl-shaped container used for drinking), and *evaporate* (turn from liquid to vapor). Only the definition for *cup* includes a physical description. Highly concrete words tend to be learned with greater ease and may be better retained over time. Imageability refers to the ease with which one can develop a mental image of the concept or item. Concrete nouns (*flower*) tend to be easier to visualize in contrast to mental state verbs (*thinking*).

Mental state verbs, or verbs that describe thoughts, feelings, ideas, or emotions, are also useful for instruction as they relate to cognitive processes that are not highly imageable or concrete. For example, words such as *hypothesize, predict,* and *assume* can be found across academic disciplines and frequently in academic writing. Knowledge of these terms may help students develop stronger conceptual knowledge in multiple subject areas due to improved comprehension. The following list presents some useful academic verbs and their broader categorizations that may be excellent choices for instruction. These terms tend to be more abstract than concrete and are difficult to imagine, hence explicit instruction may be merited.

Abstract Academic Verbs for Instruction

Verb Type	Examples
Activity Verbs	produce, provide, apply, form, obtain, reduce
Communication Verbs	describe, suggest, assert
Mental Verbs	consider, assume, determine, hypothesize
Causative/Occurrence/ Existence Verbs	follow, allow, require, include, involve, exist

Considering these features can be helpful for planning instruction. Terms that are highly abstract and difficult to form a mental image for may require more instruction or exposure in multiple contexts than those that are highly imageable and concrete. Concrete nouns may not even require direct or explicit instruction as they can be depicted with a visual aide. You can learn nearly all that you need to know about the meaning of many concrete nouns through routine exposure. You understand what a cup is from simply using one and hearing the name. However, often full understanding of abstract terms may require conceptual knowledge that includes recognizing how a word relates to other words. For example, to fully understand the terms "liquid, solid, and gas," one needs to know how and why they are related, and acquiring this knowledge may take years.

Synonyms

Students tend to learn synonyms for known terms with greater ease than learning terms related to novel content. This is because they can use their background knowledge to make connections between the new term and what they already know. This is an important consideration when teaching and selecting academic vocabulary. Academic vocabulary found in narratives tend to be synonyms for already known terms and are used for elaboration or description. Authors of narrative pay careful attention to varying their descriptive word choices so as to avoid repetition. Terms found in narratives tend to be related to story elements such as character traits, emotions, actions, or the setting. For example, narratives may contain sentences such as "The *tranquil* pond was *peaceful* and *serene*." *Tranquil, peaceful,* and *serene* are synonyms, so if a student understands *peaceful* in this sentence, then it would require relatively little instruction to teach *tranquil* and *serene*.

In contrast, many discipline-specific terms, such as those found in mathematics, science, or social studies, are not synonyms, but rather are conceptually related. These words are related through topical clusters where understanding one term may rely on understanding other academic terms within the cluster. For example, when learning about mixtures in science, students may need to understand and use conceptually related terms such as *dissolve, combine, substance,* and *solution*. These terms may require explicit instruction as students may not be familiar with the underlying concepts, which indicates a need to teach the concept as well as the academic vocabulary word.

TEACHING ACADEMIC VOCABULARY

There is a continuum of word learning, ranging from incidental exposure to explicit instruction. Students may learn words through indirect means such as reading a word in text or hearing it used in multiple contexts. This learning may be shallow or result in only a limited understanding. Given this, some degree of explicit instruction or direct support may be needed for students to develop robust understandings of academic vocabulary terms. Explicit instruction includes providing dictionary definitions, examples, descriptions, visual representations, synonyms/antonyms, and physical demonstrations, including gestures (Barnes & Stephens, 2019). These forms of explicit instruction align with how students learn words. Decades of research show the benefits of explicit instruction, whereby the teacher purposefully provides instruction around a target set of words (e.g., Marulis & Neuman, 2010).

The type and intensity of instruction for the selected vocabulary terms should be based on both the needs (or knowledge) of the learners, as well as the degree of difficulty of the target words. We want to focus on presenting vocabulary in rich and varied language experiences (not isolated instruction), that is strategically presented and encourages students to be strategic with their thinking. Finally, we want to promote word consciousness so students are motivated to think about, learn, and use varied vocabulary.

Visual Displays

Students tend to learn the words that they see and hear the most frequently, hence providing visual displays of target academic vocabulary terms allows students to view the words over time. Visual displays may provide a categorization of the term (triangles are shapes), include the part of speech or pronunciation guide, along with a concrete visual representation. Additionally, visual displays reinforce word learning when they are incorporated into instructional routines and games.

One type of visual display is a vocabulary word wall (see Figure 4.1), which allows students to see the words over time. When developing your word wall, make sure to include clear unembellished font that can be easily read from any place in the room, a visual representation of the word, and a categorization of the term in relation to how you are studying the word.

Figure 4.1. A Vocabulary Word Wall

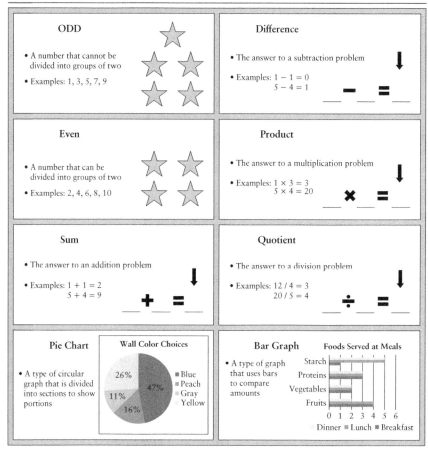

Categorization may refer to the part of speech (noun, verb, adjective), or how the word is associated with other terms in the unit of study (animal, shape, process). It can be helpful to color code the cards initially to help with distinguishing between the different categories.

Word walls can be used for many activities that promote engagement. Students can be asked to match up words based on similarities or differences. For example, a word wall focusing on animals could ask students to identify examples of carnivores or herbivores. Similarly, students can be asked to find synonyms or antonyms for target words. Students can also be asked to create categories and explain how their chosen examples demonstrate category membership. Older students may be asked to identify words based on morphological features such as words that end in –ology or –ist. Word walls can be utilized for all academic disciplines and can be used throughout the school day (see Chapter 9). They may be excellent for quick reviews of words during transition times, bathroom breaks, and so on, where students can be asked to quickly match words while waiting for other students or new activities to begin.

When you are teaching words whose meanings are embedded in complex clusters of concepts (e.g., state, country, province, county; or liquid, solid, gas), consider whether you can teach the cluster of words at one time and recognize that full understanding of some words will require conceptual learning in later grades.

Instructional Routines

Developing sets of instructional routines may be practical and useful, particularly when the routines may be incorporated across instructional settings and content areas. Instructional routines should be relatively short; you should be able to teach 5–7 words within 15 minutes. The following routine (Table 4.1) was found effective for teaching elementary students (Manyak, 2010).

Finish up this brief routine by including an activity or providing students with an open-ended question for discussion or writing. You can provide a scenario and have students decide if it fits with the target word (Theo was *dismayed* when he got exactly what he wanted for his birthday), or provide students two scenarios and ask them to explain how one fits with the target word (Theo gets exactly what he wants for his birthday or Theo doesn't get anything he wants for his birthday). This routine can be repeated for a variety of target terms across multiple content areas (see Table 4.2).

Card Sorts. Once students have been introduced to the target vocabulary terms, they may extend their understanding and use through card-sorting activities. In these activities, a pair of students is provided with several of the target vocabulary words neatly printed on card stock and several laminated

Table 4.1. Vocabulary Instructional Routine (Extended Routine)

Instructional Move	Example
Introduce the target term within a context, such as a read-aloud text.	The girl was *dismayed* when she lost her favorite bracelet.
Provide a student-friendly definition of the term.	*Dismay* means feeling sad, disappointed, or upset, usually because something has changed.
Provide examples of the word in use in other contexts.	You may feel *dismayed* when your baseball game is cancelled because of rain. Esperanza felt *dismayed* when she couldn't go on the field trip because she was sick.
Ask students to use the word.	Try to think of a time when you felt *dismayed*. Tell your shoulder partner and make sure to use the word *dismayed*.
Show an image of the word and explain how it relates to the meaning.	Use your smartboard or present images on cardstock.

Table 4.2. Vocabulary Instructional Routine for Discussion and Writing

Instructional Move	Example for the word *Toiled*
Slide 1: Show the word as used in the text and provide one to two additional examples of the word in use in familiar scenarios (classroom, community, home).	The farmer *toiled* in the field all day ensuring his crop would survive the hard climate. Shar *toiled* over the tough math problem, showing each step of her work.
Slide 2: Provide a student-friendly definition that describes and categorizes the word.	*Definition:* to have worked very hard for a long time *Categorization:* verb, action word, doing something *Synonym:* to work your fingers to the bone
Slide 3: Provide an image of the term. Ask the students how the image represents the term.	

pictures. The pictures do not need to be a concrete representation of the term, but rather may represent the feeling or gist. Students can then sort the cards according to how they match the target terms and explain their decisionmaking rationale to each other. Similarly, students may also sort cards based on which do not align with the target vocabulary word and explain their choices. TextProject has produced a wide variety of free images associated with a variety of academic topics for use with younger learners that may be useful for such activities. Having students discuss their selections and provide rationale provides another opportunity for academic talk.

The Frayer Model. The Frayer Model (Frayer et al., 1969) is a graphic organizer that can be used to support conceptual understanding. This organizer includes a definition, defining characteristics or properties of the term, and examples and nonexamples of the term. Typically, the target word is placed in the center of the page and is surrounded by four boxes that include the definition, characteristics, examples, and nonexamples (see Figure 4.2). The original graphic organizer was intended to include words, but more modern versions also include visual representations. Students may wish to draw or include photos of examples and nonexamples, and may also wish to include a visual of the target term. Completing the organizer as a class or having students work in pairs encourages discussion around the vocabulary term and may build knowledge and understanding.

Figure 4.2. Example of the Frayer Model for Representing Academic Vocabulary

DEFINITION	CHARACTERISTICS OR PROPERTIES
A change in size or shape of matter that can be reversed but does not change the composition	Material is made up of the same things before and after the change. Chemical composition is the same.

TARGET WORD

Physical Change

EXAMPLES	NONEXAMPLES
Melting ice Freezing water Cutting fingernails Condensing gas	Burning wood Baking a cake Iron rusting Combining hydrogen and oxygen

Word Consciousness. Using strategies in our vocabulary instruction may also help students to become strategic word learners who have highly developed word consciousness. Word consciousness is essentially interest in or attention to words. A student who is word conscious will actively wonder about words and seek out their meanings. They are interested in words and how they work, and tend to be motivated to learn words.

You can help to build word consciousness through talking with students in a manner that builds interest in words. Neugebauer et al. (2017) found that teachers who helped students see how a novel term is connected to their lives, and positively reinforced word use/recognition, had students who showed more general vocabulary gain over the course of 1 year of kindergarten. Asking students to find examples of the word in their lives (Do you know someone who is *sympathetic*?), or their environments (Can you find an *array* of something in your house?), can demonstrate the utility of the term and also how the term can be used in multiple contexts. Additionally, praising students for using or noticing academic vocabulary terms may build word consciousness (Wonderful job noticing our new word, *contract*! I love how you asked what *spinal* meant!). Try to repeat the target or novel word in your praise as repetition can support word learning.

CONCLUSION

Academic vocabulary may require specific and different forms of instruction than other vocabulary terms. How and when you teach academic vocabulary should be dictated by the topic of study and the students you are teaching. Remember to model how the academic vocabulary is used within contexts, particularly highlighting when academic vocabulary is used within conversations and texts. After modeling the vocabulary terms and providing descriptions, visuals, and definitions, engage your students in activities that prompt them to think about how/when the terms can be used, how they are different/similar from other terms, and how they relate to the larger unit or concept of study. When selecting instructional strategies, make sure to consider how difficult the term is to visualize, considering concreteness and imageability. Also consider if the term is a synonym for what is already known. Consider using instructional routines for teaching vocabulary and provide students with ample opportunity to use the terms in classroom activities such as card sorts and word walls. Repeated engagement in rich instructional environments is likely to lead to deep and rich understanding of academic vocabulary terms.

CHAPTER 5

Complex Syntax

Coauthored by Katherine Newman

PRIMING QUESTIONS:

1. How do you teach from and with complex syntax in your classroom?
2. Which materials and spaces do you find useful for promoting the use of complex syntax?

Syntax is the set of rules used to organize individual words into more complex ideas through the use of phrases, clauses, and sentences (Farrow et al., 2020), along with the inclusion of affixes and inflections that provide grammatical information (Vasilyeva & Waterfall, 2011). Simply put, syntax is the glue that holds words together to create larger chunks of meaning than can be conveyed through a single word. Joining words together into phrases or clauses provides more detail and creates cohesion within a text. For example, using the word *tree* alone does not evoke the same image as "the elderly willow tree near the edge of the creek whose boughs kiss the water with grace." Syntax allows us to convey the complexity that is inherent in everyday life by describing where, how, and when it was done, along with who did it (Pinker, 2013).

Syntax may be categorized by its degree of complexity, with complexity referring to the amount of information or detail provided. Typically, simple syntax contains a single thought, idea, or action, such as "the girl spoke," or "lemmings plunge." Simple syntax is used to convey meaning in either an independent clause or simple sentence containing a subject and verb. In contrast, complex syntax adds supplementary detail through the addition of multiple subjects, verbs, and descriptions, which are connected through conjunctions (e.g., "Chicks and goslings peck at the ground and squawk noisily while wandering around the barnyard"). Complex syntax may involve dependent clauses that must be attached to an independent clause (e.g., "She wore a raincoat even though it was sunny"). Complex syntax may explain or elaborate, describe a cause and effect relationship, present a timeline or location of events, or explain meanings of novel terms (Farrow et al., 2020). It plays an important role in communicating complex ideas.

Students need to have a strong grasp of complex syntax when reading academic textbooks in the later elementary grades and beyond. Bailey and Butler (2003) found that the majority of analyzed passages from science textbooks used in 5th grade had sentences ranging from 10 to 18 words, with 40% of these lengthy sentences containing complex syntax such as embedded clauses. As noted in grade-level standards, students are expected to use complex syntax in their writing as they progress in school.

DEVELOPMENT OF COMPLEX SYNTAX

Language development is a gradual process that requires input from more mature speakers (Tomasello, 2000). Young children initially produce language that is very simple, with single words standing in for entire sentences. For example, a very young child may simply say "juice" to accomplish a variety of tasks. The child may be naming the juice on the counter, requesting more juice, or responding to a question. In order to understand the full meaning of "juice," the listener must be familiar with the context in which the child is producing the word. Without the context, the meaning or intent of the communication is unclear. As infants become toddlers, the complexity of their utterances increases through the inclusion of more words. Children's speech may become less dependent on the context, "more juice!" but context is still needed to fully understand the communication. As additional words are added, sentences become more complex, allowing the ideas to be understood by someone not immediately present in the context. For example, the specificity in the utterance, "I want the pineapple juice that is in the refrigerator behind the milk, please!" is accomplished by the use of phrases and clauses that add precision.

Younger children tend to rely on simple sentences to convey meaning by using strings of independent clauses. Over time, they increasingly use dependent clauses to create more complex utterances (Nippold et al., 2005). Indeed, a key marker of syntactic growth in children is the increased inclusion of relative clauses (e.g., "under the table, before we eat dinner.") (Nippold et al., 2005). By age 5, most children are able to use relative, adverbial, and nominal clauses on occasion in conversations (see Table 5.1).

COMMON SYNTACTIC STRUCTURES

Certain features of academic language are conveyed through using complex syntax. For example, academic language is characterized by its ability to convey information in a condensed manner. This density may be achieved through cohesive devices such as coordinating or subordinating conjunctions. As we have noted, academic language may be decontextualized. Embedded clauses help one to communicate in this manner by adding clarity and precision. An academic register found in written text is more likely to combine clauses to create stronger cohesion. To create greater cohesion, precision, context, and

Table 5.1. Common and Less Common Conjunctions

Common Conjunctions	Less Common Conjunctions
And	Although
But	While
Or	Whereas
	However
	Moreover

content, we may include syntactic features such as conjunctions, embedded clauses, descriptive phrases, passive voice, and nominalizations.

Cohesive Devices

As stated, academic language conveys a considerable amount of information in a concise manner. In order to communicate complex ideas, it is necessary to use multiple clauses combined into complex sentences. This combining is frequently achieved using conjunctions, which are words that connect or coordinate words, phrases, and clauses (see Table 5.1). Many of these conjunctions are used in casual speech and may not require explicit instruction. For example, in casual language, we are likely to use *and* to join together multiple ideas or thoughts. In fact, *and* is used five times as much in oral conversation as in written texts (Lazaraton, 1992). However, less common conjunctions may require more explicit instruction. They are more typically found in printed text than in oral language.

Clauses

Clauses are groups of words that contain a subject and predicate and are found in complex or compound sentences. In academic language, clauses are used as parts of sentences to convey complexity of thought and enhanced detail. Three types of clauses are particularly useful for building academic language: relative, adverbial, and nominal (described in Table 5.2). Most 5-year-olds can produce a wide variety of clauses (Paul, 1981) but are not yet proficient or prolific in using each type. This indicates that teachers may help young students build these skills.

Passive Voice

Passive voice is a grammatical construct in which the object of the action becomes the subject of the sentence. For example, *Mistakes were made* is a classic example of passive voice in that mistakes are the subject of the sentence, rather than the person who actually made the mistakes. Passive voice

Table 5.2. Clause Types and Descriptions

Clause Type	Description	Example *(italicized)*
Relative (Adjective) Clause	Acts like an adjective and describes (modifies) a noun that comes before it	The girl *who was eating the ice cream cone* was content. The car *that was speeding down the street* was chased by the police.
Adverbial Clause	Acts like an adverb and describes (modifies) a verb. May begin with a subordinate conjunction and may describe a condition or cause	*Unless we hurry up*, we'll be late for school. *If you decide to go to the party*, I'll go with you.
Nominal Clause	Acts like a noun that can be the subject or object of a sentence. Composed of multiple words that function as a noun. Often begin with "wh" words (why, when, where, and so on)	I can never remember *where I parked the car.* My desire to eat chocolate cake every day is *why I work out so frequently.*

may be used to present information in an objective tone rather than as a result of human action. It is found in textbooks across academic disciplines and in narrative storybooks.

The syntax of written text may be more challenging than common speech due to the increased presence of passive sentences (van Kleeck et al., 2006). The ability to understand and use passive sentences is developed in the later preschool years, and children can be helped to master this syntactic form by hearing it relatively often. Vasilyeva et al. (2006) found that children who heard stories with a high concentration of passives better understood sentences with passives than those who heard stories without them. This study demonstrates the value of using books to help children to learn syntax.

Nominalizations

Nominalizations involve changing a verb, adjective, short phrase, or sentence into a noun or noun phrase. Nominalizations increase the density and precision of language. For example, the sentence "You may get a rash where you applied the lotion to your skin" becomes, "A rash may appear at the application site." In this example, *where you applied* is nominalized to become *application site.* Nominalizations may be easy to spot as many end in *-tion.* As in the previous example, nominalization may eliminate the agent of the action, making the language less personal. This depersonalization is typical in science and social studies texts as it creates the illusion of an agentless action that may appear more neutral and unquestionable. *The deforestation of the Amazon rainforest* does not include the agent who performed the deforestation. In this example, note the subtle rhetorical effect of this construction: An authoritative voice describes the process and avoids assigning responsibility to any particular agent. Discussing the meaning conveyed by *how* ideas are communicated with students can help them become more sensitive to the nuances conveyed through language.

Embedded Questions

An embedded question is a question that appears within another question or a declarative statement. Examples of embedded questions are "In your opinion, *who is the better candidate*?" and "I don't know *what the weather will be tomorrow*." Academic language may contain embedded questions that pose comprehension problems. Students may understand common questions such as "Where do you think the fins on a dolphin are?" This type of syntax is typical of everyday, casual conversation. In contrast, this question may be posed differently in a classroom where an academic register is spoken: "What is your best estimate of where the fins are located on a dolphin?" Here, the actual question is about the location of the fins, but it is embedded within another question asking for an estimate. Not only are there academic word choices (best estimate) that may pose challenges, but there are also differences in how the question is posed. The question is now embedded within the second clause (*where the fins are located*) rather than being foregrounded as in the casual talk example. Students may struggle to determine what the question is in the second example because two question words are embedded (*what* and *where*). Students may know where a dolphin's fins are located but may not understand the question, which may result in an inaccurate response. These types of embedded questions may be particularly challenging for ELLs.

COMPLEX SYNTAX IN ACADEMIC TEXTS

Classroom texts include a variety of complex syntax forms that differ across subject areas. These grammatical patterns reflect the purpose of the text and the register associated with each academic subject (Fang, 2006). For example, the purpose of a storybook is to entertain and engage readers by creating an imaginary world that they cannot see or touch. The language found in storybooks conveys information about setting, actions, and characters' emotions using complex syntax. In the following storybook example, two embedded clauses expand the amount of information contained in one sentence by linking a character's action to her emotions about a past event: "She touched the medal and talked sadly of the big brother (1) she had loved (2) who had gone to the war and never returned" (Fox, 1984). In addition, readers must link the second clause describing who went to war to a character introduced earlier (*the big brother*), as opposed to the clause immediately preceding it (*she had loved*). Students rarely encounter sentences so densely packed with informative clauses in everyday conversation.

Table 5.3. Complex Syntax in Texts

Text Genre	Text Example	Complex Syntax Features
Language Arts: Storybook	*Even though* her patch was old, it fit right in. Luke was barely in position when *the next ball flew past and* the catcher yelled, "Out!"	Cohesive device: abstract conjunction Embedded clause
Science	When the *transformation* is complete, the Monarch emerges from the chrysalis with wings that are too damp for flight. The term "band" *is used* when talking about a small group of caribou. Sometimes in the spring, caribou migrate to the mountains where it is too cold for mosquitoes. (Richter & Richter, 2000)	Nominalization Passive voice Multiclause sentence that conveys a logical relationship
Social Studies	*The type of food people ate and the kind of houses they built* depended on the climate and the wildlife of the area where they lived. When the new settlers came, the Cherokee stopped using stone and bone tools. (Roop & Roop, 1998)	Abstract noun phrase Multiclause sentence that conveys a cause–effect or temporal relationship

Science texts often use nominalizations and conjunctions to present dense information in cohesive chains across several paragraphs. For example, an informational text about insect life cycles describes how a caterpillar *transforms* into a butterfly while inside a chrysalis. In a subsequent paragraph, the same complex process is presented as a one-word nominalization, condensing prior information and building cohesion: *When the transformation is complete, the Monarch emerges from the chrysalis with wings that are too damp for flight.* Listeners must recall the complex process that *transformation* refers to while unpacking new content in the latter part of the sentence.

Over the course of a school day, teachers use multiple texts with academic registers that may pose comprehension challenges for young learners (see Table 5.3). Awareness of the complex syntax found in subject area texts will enable teachers to plan activities that help students understand complex texts as well as engage in related oral and written activities.

MODELING AND INSTRUCTING

Complex syntax is useful for increasing the cohesion and density of language, but it may be challenging for younger students or those who have less experience with these grammatical forms. The good news is that instruction focused on complex syntax can be beneficial. Simply modeling complex syntax through oral language or reading aloud texts is helpful for students' production and use of complex syntax (Huttenlocher et al., 2002). Instruction focused on teaching about clauses has also been related to children's reading comprehension gains (Phillips, 2014).

Particular instructional settings require or provide different types of complex syntax, and some instructional settings contain greater amount of complex syntax than others (Dickinson et al., 2014). In order for children to become proficient users of more complex syntax structures, they must be exposed to sufficient doses (Tomasello, 2000). This means that modeling complex syntax is essential for producing competent speakers and writers who use complex syntax in their speech and as they write.

Modeling complex syntax in your speech may also help students develop deeper understandings of how concepts and ideas are connected. Simple syntax can convey information in streamlined explanations, "Our unit is about animals. Animals live in certain habitats. Their food source is near their homes." However, presenting information in such small, disconnected chunks may not show how the ideas are connected. More complex syntax can show the interrelationships between these ideas, "Animals choose to live in habitats that contain their food source, which allows them to survive with greater ease and prevent extinction." This example shows the cause and effect relationship (living in a habitat with food sources causes greater survival rates), which deepens students' understanding of animal habitats. Additionally, the inclusion of the nominalization, *extinction*, helps students focus on specificity. While the example containing complex syntax has a higher cognitive load in terms of student processing, it may build processing skills when teachers provide appropriate scaffolding. This may also assist students with understanding complex syntax within printed text.

Students may benefit from first hearing complex syntax modeled by you or through reading a text (together or independently), then being supported using these syntactic forms through scaffolded activities, before being asked to produce complex syntax independently. Many of the activities described next involve both modeling and engaging students in talking and writing with complex syntax. The earlier strategies tend to provide more support through modeling, while the later strategies encourage more student production.

Modeling During Read-Alouds

Younger students who are not yet reading independently may benefit from read-alouds of academic texts that include fiction, nonfiction, and hybrid texts. These texts need not be lengthy, as the goal is to transmit academic content in academic language. Shorter nonfiction texts, such as those published by *National Geographic*, may contain appropriate academic content couched in academic language. These texts may be read aloud in a single session. During the read-aloud, you may wish to point out how the authors use language in particular ways to convey information. This does not necessarily mean naming specific grammatical features such as noun phrases, but rather discussing the language choices and how they create clarity. For example, the following text on hibernation contains complex syntax that creates cohesion: "Brown fat makes heat, which helps to protect a hibernating animal's organs, such as the brain, while it sleeps through the cold winter" (Kosara, 2012). While reading aloud, it's important to ask questions to ensure students understand who, what, where, and how. For this example, you may wish to ask these questions:

- *What* organ is protected by brown fat? (the brain)
- *How* does brown fat protect the hibernator? (it makes heat)
- *Why* does the animal need to stay warm? (the winters are cold)

Use the illustrations to support meaning, particularly in nonfiction science texts where graphics may present additional information.

Facilitating Syntactic Awareness

It also is important to develop awareness at both the word (lexical) and sentence (syntax) level in order to promote students' use and understanding of language (Deacon & Kieffer, 2018). Syntactic awareness refers to a degree of alertness to how phrases, clauses, and sentences are used to convey information in more complex or simple manners. Students who pay more attention to the wording of written or spoken language may think more carefully about how to construct meaning through their language choices.

One means for promoting syntactic awareness is through a revised model of the Initiate-Respond-Evaluate (IRE) sequence (Heller, 2015). In an IRE sequence, the teacher usually initiates the interaction by posing a question (Initiate), to which the student responds (Respond), followed by an evaluation by the teacher/adult (Evaluate). The IRE sequence is commonly employed when the teacher asks a question that may have a limited number of appropriate responses ("What color is the sky?"), such that the evaluation may denote the correctness of the child's response. To help students develop syntactic awareness, this sequence may be refocused such that the evaluation focuses on the syntax utilized within the child's response. The following IRE exchange focuses on the grammatical form of the answer in addition to acknowledging an appropriate response. Note how the teacher focuses on the student's choice of words.

> *Teacher:* Why do we need to recycle?
> *Student:* We should recycle because it reduces the amount of trash we make.

Teacher: Nice thinking! I like how you explained your response using the word "because"!

Discussing Mental States with Clauses

Including mental state verbs, which are verbs that express thoughts, memories, knowledge, feelings, or ideas (Barnes & Dickinson, 2018), may naturally promote the use of complex syntax. One strategy is to *model use* of target constructs. When working with preschoolers or kindergarteners, you may model nominal clauses through instruction targeted at emotions, particularly focusing on asking students to identify when they feel a certain emotion. For example, you may model the following response including a nominal clause, "I feel happy *when I play outside in the sunshine.*" When you are intentionally modeling use you can then *scaffold use* by asking students when they feel happy, providing a sentence stem if necessary: "When do you feel happy? You can start by saying, 'I feel happy when . . .'" These simple conversations may help students increase their use of nominal clauses. Similarly, you can model the use of adverbial and relative clauses to provide more detail and precision. Modeling and questioning may be helpful strategies for building proficiency. You may ask a student to help gather supplies from the classroom and use a relative clause to distinguish the item from other similar items, "Sophie, will you please collect the folders *that are red*?" When a student asks for a general item, you may respond, "Which one would you like? You can begin your sentence by saying 'I would like the one that . . .'"

Conversing in Small Groups

Small group settings may also be ideal for modeling and evoking clauses. Conversation stations may be incorporated in centers. Conversation stations ask students to focus on having oral conversations so they are speaking and listening carefully (Bond & Wasik, 2009). Initially, you may wish to sit at the conversation station to help students engage in specific conversations that include complex syntax. As students become more proficient, you may withdraw your support and include other students or classroom aids or volunteers. Providing sentences stems and frames, complete with visual aids, may be supportive. Students may play Guess Who at the conversation station, too. Table 5.4 highlights possible topics for conversation stations that may evoke the use of complex syntax.

Content area instruction in elementary school includes complex syntactic structures, particularly clauses. In mathematics, the teacher may introduce different shapes and use relative clauses to provide precise description, "*The triangle is the shape that has three sides and three angles.*" This sentence provides a categorization (shape), while also including details

Table 5.4. Sentence Stems for Promoting Complex Syntax

Topic	Sentence Stems	Visual Aids
Emotions	I feel ____ when I ____.	Emoticons, photos of family members, images of toys, and so on.
Character traits	The (character) is the one that ____.	Images of characters from a recently read text, list of adjectives, list of events from story
Past events	Last weekend I went to the ___ where I did _____.	Student journals, calendar of community events, images of local parks, attractions, or landmarks

that show how a triangle is different from other shapes (has three sides and three angles). Students may then use the conversation to sort objects or images into different categories and provide descriptions of the characteristics that involve relative clauses. You may wish to provide students with three-dimensional objects or images to sort, as well as a sorting grid that includes the categories. Students may be asked to sort shapes, landforms, geographical features, parts of speech, and odd/even numbers.

Creating Cohesion

Word walls may be particularly useful for teaching conjunctions that create cohesion in language (see Figure 5.1). Divide your word wall into three sections. On one side, you can list the target conjunctions that you will be focusing on in your instruction (because, although, while). In the middle column, list how each conjunction is used (provides an explanation, tells when something happened, and so on). The final column can provide an example of the conjunction in use. Initially, you'll want to place the explanation adjacent to the target term, but as students become more proficient, you may wish to mix them up and have students match. You may want to remove the examples with time and familiarity. These words can then be used to join clauses or phrases you have posted. Clauses or phrases can be written on sentence strips with Velcro on the back and placed in a bin near the word wall. Students may use these sentence strips to create more complex (or funny) ideas through incorporating the conjunctions. This activity may be particularly useful in a science or social studies class when exploring cause and effect.

Word webs can be a fabulous way for students to make connections between words and ideas and can be used as a springboard for promoting the use of complex syntax. Begin your word web activity by reading a short informational text. Select the key academic terms from the text and place them in circles on your word web. For example, in a text about wolves,

Figure 5.1. Conjunction Word Wall

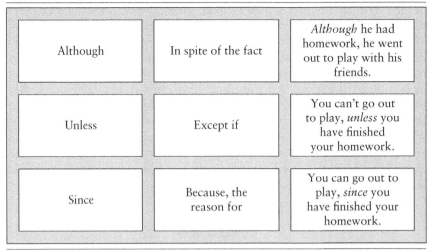

Although	In spite of the fact	*Although* he had homework, he went out to play with his friends.
Unless	Except if	You can't go out to play, *unless* you have finished your homework.
Since	Because, the reason for	You can go out to play, *since* you have finished your homework.

words such as *predator, prey, packs*, and *lope* would be perfect. Make sure to include nouns, verbs, adjectives, and adverbs. Next, engage the students in a discussion of how these terms are connected, drawing arrows between the key academic terms and writing the connections above these lines. For example, "The predator hunts the prey." This simple sentence can then be made more complex by linking it to other key words or adding in descriptive words or phrases. Consider asking students how, when, where, and so on, as a means for promoting syntax. "Why does the predator hunt prey?" may elicit the more complicated response, "The predator hunts his prey for food when it is hungry." Digital organizers such as Kidspiration can be particularly useful for this activity. Following the completion of the word web, students may then be invited to create an audio recording of their word web, highlighting the many connections between concepts they have developed with the inclusion of complex syntax. Older students may be asked to write a paragraph using the complex syntax from their word webs.

Composing Academic Definitions

Academic definitions, such as those found in dictionaries, are a specific form of academic language that include complex syntax, typically following the framework "an __ is something (*class*) which (*attribute: property, location, composition*)." For example, a dictionary definition of *poodle* is an intelligent canine (class) with curly hair (attribute) that does not shed (property) and can be grouped into three sizes (attribute). *Poodle* is the term being defined, canine is the categorization/class, intelligent, curly hair, nonshedding, and three sizes are differentiating attributes.

Using this framework can help students build cohesion and complexity in their writing. Students should be assigned or allowed to select an item to describe based on the current unit of study (shapes, animals, decomposers). They should create a definition using this framework; for example, a sand dune is a landform (class) that is made of sand (property), was created by the wind (attribute/composition), and is found near a large body of water or in a desert (location). After students have created their definitions, they may play guessing games, such as 20 Questions. Students should ask about the categorization, properties, and defining features rather than try to guess what the target word is (*What does it do? Where can it be found? Is it round?*). The answers to the questions should be found within the definition. Once the target word has been properly guessed, the student should share the dictionary definition with the group.

CONCLUSION

You can incorporate many fun and engaging activities that encourage students to understand and use complex syntax into your daily instructional routine. Remember that students must first hear complex syntax, so strive to model complex syntax across a variety of instructional settings. Additionally, keep in mind that the type of syntax used in different text genres and instructional settings may vary. This means you have many opportunities to teach from and with complex syntax across your instructional day. Reading different genres of texts, exploring definitions, and creating opportunities to add complexity may help students see the utility of complex syntax and encourage them to incorporate this aspect of academic language into their language routines.

CHAPTER 6

Academic Discourse

PRIMING QUESTIONS:

1. What are the features of academic discourse for PreK-3 classrooms?
2. How do these discourses prepare students to read and write a variety of texts?
3. Which activities, structures, and scaffolds might increase the knowledge and use of academic discourse in your classroom?

As discussed in earlier chapters, we are defining three important levels of academic language: vocabulary, syntax, and discourse. Discourse is the highest, the most complex, and the level with which students and even skilled writers struggle. Discourse is spoken or written language in use, with language features and forms that signal the role of the speaker or writer and match the purpose or activity. Thus, academic discourse is the specialized use of language in the social context of schools and classrooms.

FEATURES OF ACADEMIC DISCOURSE

Writers and readers both influence the way that written academic discourses are structured, and speakers and listeners (or conversational partners) both influence the way that oral academic discourses unfold in the classroom. The features and structures of academic discourse vary based on the social purposes for language use (Schleppegrell, 2004). Notable characteristics of academic discourse are the degree of contextualization, tone, stance, and genre used.

Contextualization

The degree of contextualization of academic discourse differs from typical casual discourse used in nonacademic settings. Casual interpersonal discourse is primarily focused on the shared immediate context and knowledge and familiarity between the interlocutors. Family members often talk about present happenings in the immediate context, and friends write or text about common experiences or shared acquaintances. In contrast, academic discussions or texts are not all about the here and now, but rather include decontextualized language about events, people, and things that are far removed or not visibly present (Rowe, 2013; Snow, 1983). In textbooks and classrooms, the topics are often abstract ideas and concepts, imagined stories, or past or future events. Academic discourses often include talk about language and thinking, such as questioning the meaning of a phrase or explaining why you made a particular prediction. These topics lead to abstract uses of language, where the speaker must assume some prior knowledge on the part of the listener and also provide clear and specific information. For example, casual oral stories tend to include many pronouns (*We* went to that fire station. *They* had two dogs *there*.), because the shared context allows for easier comprehension by the listener. In comparison, oral and written academic narratives use fewer pronoun referents for clarity about events in another time or place (Dad and *I* went to the fire station around the corner from *our* house. The firefighters had two dogs at the station.).

Tone

Academic discourses tend to take on a formal tone, which is the voice or style of the speaker or writer. This formal tone signals the expertise and knowledge of the speaker. In a classroom discussion, a formal tone may arise from interaction "rules" where students contribute in a formal manner by taking turns, raising hands, and responding to one another's contributions. This differs from casual discussions where speakers may jump in and interrupt one another, offering short responses that require shared knowledge or familiarity. Likewise, texts used in classrooms, particularly textbooks or informational texts, feature a formal tone that establishes the authority of the writer through elements such as use of third person and proper names. The formal tone also features metacognitive or mental state talk, where speakers use abstract language to communicate ideas and higher level reasoning (e.g., "I wonder what will happen if . . ." or "I agree with Jacqui because . . . "). At the same time, the formal tone of academic discourse writing is concise, ideas are stated efficiently, and a considerable amount of information is communicated in as few words as possible (Snow & Uccelli, 2009).

Stance

Stance is the manner in which interlocutors (the people participating in the conversation) are positioned in an interaction, whether as speaker and listener or writer and reader. The stance of the speaker or writer in academic discourse indicates perspective and assumes some shared knowledge or effectively communicates necessary background information. In academic discourse there is a need to be explicit about the credibility of the information that you are sharing and to signal authority or knowledge with specificity or references to texts and other sources of information (Snow & Uccelli, 2009). A teacher's instructional stance in facilitating the classroom discourse establishes norms and patterns of interactions, such as a traditional lecture or dialogic teaching. These patterns prescribe when and how students and teachers will talk in the classroom, what counts as academic discourses, and what the rules are in discourse for various purposes (Soter et al., 2008). In academic texts, the author's stance typically indicates authority, informing, persuading, or entertaining the reader at a distance—as a nonpresent audience.

Genre

Genre is the function or form of language, including the rhetorical structures used for different purposes. Particular genres comprise the oral and written discourses of the classroom, where language is used to perform different functions (Halliday, 1978). In the classroom, language functions for numerous abstract and inferential purposes. Language is used for the purposes of informing, entertaining, explaining, summarizing, persuading, arguing, or inquiring. These genres translate into oral discourse genres such as story retellings, mathematical explanations, and scientific arguments; as well as text genres such as informational texts, folk tales, persuasive letters, and reading responses. Each genre has specific features of language and structure (Snow, 1983), and students will be expected to compose and comprehend texts with a variety of these functions as they move through school (Uccelli et al., 2015b). Text genre and related features are an increasing focus of early childhood curriculum and standards.

Thoughtfully incorporating academic discourse into early childhood classrooms is especially important for students with disabilities that impact communication, such as autism spectrum disorder or specific language impairments. Modeling of and explicit instruction in academic discourse features is particularly helpful for these students as they are learning the mechanics and the pragmatic uses of language. It is also critical for English learners who need many opportunities to learn and practice academic language in English.

Oral and written academic discourse is complex, and learners continue to develop their facility with these discourses throughout their academic careers. You may wonder whether your students are capable of engaging in rigorous academic discourse in pre-K through 3rd grade. In fact, young children employ many types of academic discourses in classroom discussions and when reading and writing for academic purposes (Gallagher, 2016; Lucero, 2014; Scheele et al., 2012). You can support your students' abilities to engage in oral academic discourse, as well as reading and writing academic texts. Building these skills during the early childhood years will provide a foundation for your students' academic success for years to come.

Above all, you should have high expectations for your students' ability to engage in and acquire academic discourse.

ACADEMIC DISCOURSE IN EARLY CHILDHOOD CLASSROOMS

Prekindergarten through 3rd-grade students can engage in academic discussions, read and compose academic texts, and build metalinguistic awareness around features of academic discourse with appropriate support. Different settings and topics may be useful for modeling and teaching different forms of academic discourse. For example, sharing time (see Chapter 7) is a common activity in early childhood classrooms where students learn to orally narrate and inform their peers (Cazden, 2001; Michaels, 1981). Sharing time is an introduction to academic presentation and may be a setting where students present personal opinions, explanations, or arguments. Students are apprenticed into the "rules" of this discourse format by their teachers and classmates, but also may require some direct instruction in academic discourse norms. Science explorations provide a context for students to learn how to construct scientific arguments (see Chapter 9). Scientific argumentation requires students to make predictions, share observations, or draw connections between cause-and-effect relationships while also engaging with others' ideas. Teachers may model these discourse practices, strategically question students, and structure discussions around hands-on explorations of science phenomenon so students learn to share their thinking with specific evidence from observations and prior knowledge (Hand et al., 2016; Sandoval et al., 2019). Likewise, read-alouds, particularly dialogic shared book reading, has a set of normative expectations: The teacher reads the text but pauses to make comments and ask questions (Barnes et al., 2017; Beck & McKeown, 2001; Pollard-Durodola et al., 2015). The questions may be literal or inferential, on a continuum of contextualization. Students may respond not only to the teacher, but to the ideas of their classmates as they engage in a true dialogue about the text.

In group discussions, teachers can set the expectations that talk is rigorous, respectful of community norms, and accountable to knowledge and text (Michaels et al., 2008). When you facilitate conversations, you can make particular moves to increase the cognitive and linguistic demands of the discourse. Early childhood teachers who take a dialogic instructional stance, asking open-ended questions, being responsive to students, and elaborating on topics to extend the conversation, have been associated with stronger language and literacy outcomes for students (Cabell et al., 2015; Dickinson & Smith, 1994; Massey et al., 2008). Allowing students to respond to one another in authentic discussions of academic content leads to more rigorous discourse and deeper understanding of the content

(Michaels et al., 2008). Rigorous academic discourse features a balance between teacher and student talk, where students are actively engaged in constructing knowledge.

These patterns of academic discourse stand in contrast to traditional classroom discourse. In a transmission-oriented instructional stance, teachers would typically adopt positioning as the main purveyor of knowledge and director of discussion topics. Teachers would facilitate discourse by posing an initial question (*initiate*), inviting a student response (*respond*), and then providing evaluation or feedback on that response (*evaluate*; Cazden, 2001). This IRE format privileges a "known" or desired answer(s) by the teacher, and it may be occasionally useful in reviewing content or background information. However, this pattern requires students to perform a "verbal display" that may be unfamiliar and culturally incongruent for many young students when they enter school (van Kleeck, 2014). Traditional discourse patterns do not allow students to engage in an authentic discourse where they collaboratively build knowledge and practice persuading, evaluating, informing, questioning, and explaining. Instead, participation norms where students engage in a variety of talk formats and use language for a variety of purposes increases the linguistic and cognitive demand of classroom discourse and prepares students to read and write academic texts.

Oral Discourses

Students learn to use language in particular ways in the classroom to accomplish academic tasks. Academic discourses are more formal than the typical casual conversation outside of the classroom. Examples of academic discourses used in early childhood classrooms include presentation, argumentation, prediction, and explanation (see the following list for more examples). Each requires certain patterns between the speaker and listeners. You may set up routines and structures to facilitate and scaffold student practice with these discourse functions. A language-rich classroom should include intentional opportunities to practice these academic discourses through one-on-one and small-group conversations, large-group discussions and sharing time, and instructional interactions such as interactive shared reading.

Oral Discourse Genres in Early Childhood Classrooms

Genre	Examples
Argument	A class debates the best way to solve an addition problem. Several students argue that using connecting blocks works best because they can check their work; several others counter that drawing is more efficient and also allows them to check their work.

Genre	Examples
Cause and Effect	During a physical science exploration on sound waves, students identify what causes a sound when a rubber band is plucked (vibrations) and how smaller or larger "plucks" change the sound.
Compare and Contrast	Students use a Venn diagram to compare and contrast versions of *Cinderella* from different cultural traditions.
Discussion	A small group of students discuss a passage about supply and demand, identifying content they found interesting and what they would still like to know.
Elaboration	In a dramatic play center, a child shares with their teacher that they are "cooking dinner." The teacher probes for more specific information, and the child elaborates, "For dinner we're having spaghetti and green beans."
Explanation	One student demonstrates for her classmates how she sorted objects by attributes. She explains she could have sorted by shape but there were many shapes, so she decided to sort by color to have fewer categories.
Narration	During sharing time, students are invited to narrate a story about a time they met a new friend.
Prediction	Before the teacher reads aloud the next book in a series by a favorite author, a student predicts that the characters will encounter a similar series of events based on their understanding of the plot patterns in these books.
Problem Solving	On the playground, there are only three balls to share among the class. A group of students propose several solutions and finally agree that three groups of students will have the balls for the first half of recess, and the rest of the students will have the balls for the second half of recess.
Retelling	In a partner discussion activity, students share with a friend about a book they read that day, retelling each of the major plot events.
Sequencing	The class engages in a shared writing activity in which they list the procedures for a scientific exploration they just completed. Students list steps in order and the teacher writes them down, using words such as *first*, *next*, and *last*.

Some specific discourses are featured in the disciplines, or content areas. Examples include explaining strategies for solving a math problem, presenting a book talk or book review in a language arts activity, or engaging in argumentation in a science lesson. Each of these specific discourse types has a particular academic function and features a degree of decontextualization, formal tone, and speaker and listener stance.

Here is an example of academic discourse in a 2nd-grade math lesson. One student, Adriana, is explaining how she solved a math problem, while her classmates listen and respond.

> *Adriana:* First, I added the ones digits. Seven plus 4 equals 11. That is what these Xs represent. But 11 is more than 10 so I circled 10 of them here. Now I have 10 and 1.
> *Maya:* I think it should be 12. There's another 1 over there.
> *Adriana:* No. . . . sorry. That was just a mistake. I'll erase it. See here it's only 11, 10, and 1.
> *Justin:* Okay, but how did you end up with 41?
> *Adriana:* We had the two tens in 27 and one ten in 14 over here. So, two tens and one ten is three tens, plus this new ten is four tens. Forty. Forty-one.

Notice how Adriana and her classmates engage in a formal academic conversation that demonstrates facility with both the content (two-digit addition) and discourse (explanation, questioning, providing suggestions). Inherent in this interaction is also the students' use of specific academic vocabulary and complex syntax. It is unlikely that Adriana and her classmates came to school knowing how to engage in academic explanations and questioning. Their teacher has intentionally taught and scaffolded their knowledge of and facility with this type of academic discourse through direct instruction and meaningful opportunities to practice.

Facilitating Oral Discourse

Teaching children to use academic discourse in the early childhood classroom requires an approach that gradually releases responsibility to students. As the teacher, you can begin by modeling the discourses typical of classroom talk. You may "think aloud" during reading, using language to make predictions, compare and contrast characters in a narrative, or articulate cause and effect in an informational text. When discussing books or academic content, pose and answer inferential, analytic questions with a formal tone. Call attention to the features of your language by naming them and using repetition to increase students' familiarity with the language patterns. You may use other models too, including videos of children and adults engaged in academic discourses.

Figure 6.1. Teacher–Student Academic Conversation

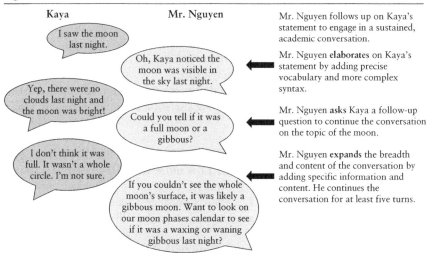

Conversations offer an opportunity for guided practice, particularly when you engage with one student or a small group of students. Academic conversations with a teacher give students a chance to practice with a more skilled conversation partner. Find opportunities to talk with individuals or small groups of students each day, during centers, small group instruction, or informal times such as snack or recess. Follow the child's lead when possible, capitalizing on their ideas or topics of interest to engage them in extended discourse. Demonstrate active listening by tuning into a child's contributions and responding by *elaborating* on their utterance, *expanding* the topic, and *asking* follow-up questions (see Figure 6.1 for an example). It is particularly important to work toward a balance of teacher and student talk, to give students opportunities to "take up" the topic and make significant contributions to the conversation. Strive for five back-and-forth turns with individual students to build their ability to engage in extended conversations on a topic.

You can establish discourse routines through the physical classroom environment and structured opportunities to practice with peers. Set up opportunities for students to play or engage in centers activities in groups of two to four, including activities that require discussion and collaboration. Centers may include print or visual discussion prompts to help students engage in discourse around the content or activity. Students may be seated at tables or grouped for certain activities where they engage in small-group discussions with specified roles or routines. Engage in whole-group discussions in a shared area such as a carpet where students can easily see and hear one another. Establish discussion norms for large groups, including raising hands but also perhaps having ways to call on peers, a "sharing stick" that signals who has the floor, and active listening expectations. Build sharing time into

Figure 6.2. Second-Grade Whole-Class Literature Discussion Anchor Chart

Text Discussions

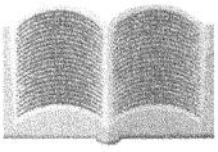

- I wonder. . .
- Where did you find that in the text?
- That reminds me of. . .
- I agree with _____ because. . .
- I disagree with _____ because. . .
- Let me think about that for a minute.
- So what you'are saying is. . .
- Can you tell me more?
- What is most important?
- How do you know?

class meetings to practice presentation and oral storytelling to practice narratives in preparation for writing. Teachers may also have students rehearse different discourse structures, such as conducting a fishbowl-style practice of problem-solving discussions, where some students engage in the discourse while the rest of the class observes. Provide explicit guidelines for peer-to-peer interactions such as asking questions or providing feedback to a classmate (see Figure 6.2). Build a classroom environment with tools such as anchor charts featuring norms for discourse or discussion prompts for different purposes.

Explicit teaching is also needed for participation in academic discourse to build knowledge and construct meaning. A number of existing instructional approaches or frameworks provide teachers with resources for facilitating strong classroom discourse. For example, *Accountable Talk* is a well-researched discourse framework that can be adapted across grade levels and content areas to foster engaged and rigorous academic discourse in the classroom (Michaels et al., 2016). *Text Talk* (Beck & McKeown, 2001) provides a framework for analytical, dialogic discussions of shared texts to co-construct meaning with primary grade students. *Literature Circles* (Daniels, 2002) or similar book club–style student text discussion groups can be implemented as early as kindergarten. These approaches build students, literal and inferential comprehension of texts while simultaneously building their facility with academic discourse and participation in a learning community.

As your students become more familiar and facile with academic discourse in classroom oral language, they can simultaneously build knowledge of academic discourse in written texts. In fact, there are clear connections between the uses of academic language in talk and text, as both modes often use the same forms and functions. As students listen to narratives read aloud and practice oral storytelling, they can learn to read and write narrative texts. As students learn to argue and explain their positions on academic topics, they can read and compose opinion texts. As students learn to inform and share knowledge in classroom discussions, they can begin to read and write informational texts.

Text Genres

Another goal in early childhood education is to learn the discourse features of various types of text. While most written academic discourse features formal tone, instructional stance, and decontextualized language, there are a variety of specific text genres with corresponding functions, features, and forms. When familiar with the characteristics of text genres, students will have stronger listening and reading comprehension and be able to compose higher quality texts. Each text genre typically features particular structures, but also uses particular vocabulary and syntax patterns. You should expose students to a variety of texts to build their familiarity with the genre, then explicitly teach the features of the genre.

Before students can read a wide range of challenging texts on their own, teachers can expose them to a variety of text genres through read-aloud and discussion. You can choose high-quality children's literature from a variety of genres, especially narrative and informational texts. The CCSS (National Governor's Association, 2010) and similar learning standards highlight the relative importance of these two genres (see Table 6.1). The shift toward more informational texts can help address the relative dearth of those texts from early childhood classrooms (Pentimonti et al., 2010; Yopp & Yopp, 2012). As your students move through the pre-K through 3rd-grade years and beyond, they should be increasingly able to read a variety of texts on their own and benefit from familiarity with genre features.

Relatedly, writing standards and curriculum are focused primarily on three modes: narrative, informational, and opinion texts. Beginning in kindergarten, students are expected to begin writing texts that incorporate each of these modes, and therefore need instruction in the discourse features of various modes of writing, such as the structure and organization of a narrative text or the author's authoritative stance in informational writing. By integrating reading and writing instruction with a variety of text types each serves the other.

Early childhood classroom instruction includes a range of specific genres that include a variety of modes and types of texts. For example, magazines, poetry, science observations, book reports, how-to instructions, textbooks, math story problems, definitions, and even test questions are specific text types with specific discourse features that students will be exposed to and begin to read and write during the early childhood years.

Table 6.1. Examples of Discourse Connections in National Standards

Content Area	Standards
CCSS Reading	R.1: Read closely to determine what the text says explicitly and to make logical inferences from it; cite specific textual evidence when writing or speaking to support conclusions drawn from the text.
	R.5: Analyze the structure of texts, including how specific sentences, paragraphs, and larger portions of the text (e.g., a section, chapter, scene, or stanza) relate to each other and the whole.
CCSS Writing	W.1: Write arguments to support claims in an analysis of substantive topics or texts using valid reasoning and relevant and sufficient evidence.
	W.2: Write informative/explanatory texts to examine and convey complex ideas and information clearly and accurately through the effective selection, organization, and analysis of content.
CCSS Speaking and Listening	SL.4: Present information, findings, and supporting evidence such that listeners can follow the line of reasoning and the organization, development, and style are appropriate to task, purpose, and audience.
	SL.6: Adapt speech to a variety of contexts and communicative tasks, demonstrating command of formal English when indicated or appropriate.
CCSS Language	L.3: Apply knowledge of language to understand how language functions in different contexts, to make effective choices for meaning or style, and to comprehend more fully when reading or listening.
CCSS Mathematics Practices	MP.3: Construct viable arguments and critique the reasoning of others.
NGSS Life Sciences	K-LS1-1: Use observations to describe patterns of what plants and animals (including humans) need to survive.
	3-LS3-2: Use evidence to support the explanation that traits can be influenced by the environment.
NGSS Earth and Space Sciences	K-ESS2-2: Construct an argument supported by evidence for how plants and animals (including humans) can change the environment to meet their needs.
NGSS Physical Sciences	2-PS1-3: Make observations to construct an evidence-based account of how an object made of a small set of pieces can be disassembled and made into a new object.
NGSS Engineering and Technology Sciences	K-2-ETS1-1: Ask questions, make observations, and gather information about a situation people want to change to define a simple problem that can be solved through the development of a new or improved object or tool.

Text Genre Instruction

As an early childhood teacher, you can greatly influence your students' knowledge of and familiarity with the academic discourses in texts. One of the most important strategies is to facilitate and encourage wide reading of a variety of text genres. You can intentionally choose a variety of text genres and structures for read-alouds, other instruction, and your classroom library. While reading with students, you can highlight text structures and features, and you can engage students in discussion about complex ideas and concepts in the texts.

Prekindergarten and kindergarten students love interactive texts, including the *Cook in a Book* series by Phaidon Press. These texts demonstrate procedural writing in the style of a recipe, while also featuring colorful illustrations and interactive elements. Note the use of discourse markers specific to this genre in *Tacos! An Interactive Recipe Book* (illustrated by Lotta Nieminen, 2017):

> Step 1: Use the first cutting board and knife to cut the chicken into cubes and toss them in a bowl with the spices.
> ½ teaspoon of cumin
> ½ teaspoon of ancho chili
> ¾ teaspoon of salt
> Cover the bowl with plastic wrap and refrigerate it for 20 minutes to an hour.

The step-by-step instructions mirror a recipe or cookbook in formality, assumption of knowledge by the reader, and lists of ingredients written in phrases rather than complete sentences. Of course, the text also includes the specific vocabulary of cooking. This simple text introduces young children to the style, format, and features of procedural writing.

During read-alouds or small group reading lessons, call attention to the features of the text genres. While reading fairytales and other types of traditional literature that have predictable elements, help students notice the common plot structures, types of characters, and refrains such as "once upon a time" and "happily ever after." While reading informational texts, note the formal tone, authoritative stance by the author, organization by topic, and special text features like photographs, charts, tables, and glossaries.

Writing instruction is another context for building student knowledge of academic text genres. In both formal and informal writing instruction, you can teach the discourse features of particular genres while engaging students in writing for authentic purposes. Prekindergarten and kindergarten students may write grocery lists in a dramatic play center, letters to friends placed in a classroom mailbox, and labels or placards for block

Figure 6.3. Primary-Grade Graphic Organizer for Features of a Science Lab Report

Name: _____

My Lab Report

| Question: | Predictions: |

Materials:

Procedures:	Observations:
1.	
2.	
3.	
4.	

or art creations. Students in grades K–3 will engage in more formal writing within each of the writing modes, benefitting from teacher instruction and the writing process. Encourage students to compose different text genres. Have them write letters to school or community leaders that include a greeting, body, and signature. Ask students to write biographies or autobiographies that are linear by time. Teach simple narrative plot structures (beginning-middle-end, problem-solution) to shape narrative construction. Integrate the elements of written discourse into content-area instruction, such as outlining the elements to include in a math explanation or features of a science lab report (see Figure 6.3). You can use model or mentor texts to connect reading and writing in particular academic text genres.

CONCLUSION

With intentionality and purpose, you as the teacher can facilitate a classroom with rigorous academic discussion, build your students' oral discourse skills, and foster students' understanding of academic text genres. The key is to incorporate varied discourse opportunities, both between you and your students and among your students, into all aspects of the school day. Young children are able to use language for a variety of academic purposes and begin to incorporate precise language and linguistic moves into their classroom discussions. These experiences, knowledge, and skills with academic discourse will prepare students for success as they continue through their academic careers.

CHAPTER 7

Mealtimes and Sharing Time

PRIMING QUESTIONS:

1. Do you talk with your students during mealtimes or snacks in your classroom? What topics do you discuss? Who decides the topics? Who directs the conversation?
2. Do you encourage students to engage in sharing time in your classroom? Does this follow a typical show-and-tell routine, or do you vary the format?
3. How might you use nonacademic times to engage children in conversations? What would you like to learn about your students, and how might you use nonacademic times to accomplish this goal?

Settings not typically considered "academic" in nature may also provide wonderful opportunities for promoting and modeling academic language. Mealtimes, which can be any time students are eating in classrooms or with teachers and support staff, as well as sharing time, sometimes known as show-and-tell, are less formal times where adults and students have unique opportunities to bridge home and school language use.

Research has demonstrated that students learn words and develop language when there are opportunities for personalized engagement with teachers (Dickinson & Porche, 2011). This includes providing chances for students to discuss topics of personal interest that promote opportunities for developing conceptual knowledge. Additionally, students benefit from having opportunities to engage in extended discourse with a responsive partner that allows for in-depth discussion with a focus on word meanings and language in use (Harris et al., 2011). Both mealtimes and sharing time can be rich with such opportunities, particularly when adults are tuned-in and responsive. In this chapter, we will first discuss mealtimes followed by sharing time. Strategies, activities, and engagements for each setting are described in turn.

MEALTIMES

We define mealtimes as any time an adult (teacher, support staff, principal) and students eat together. This may include breakfast, lunch, and snack time in the classroom or cafeteria, or even outside on the playground. These unique times are not necessarily focused on academic content, and thus may encourage students to share stories, talk about personal interests, or ask questions. The topics may be driven by mutual interest rather than being mandated by academic curricula. This may allow teachers to be more responsive to student interests and allow them to direct the flow of the conversation. Indeed, Head Start encourages teachers to sit and eat with children in their classrooms and to engage in conversations that bridge home and school discourse styles (Administration for Children and Families, 2007). Research supports the role of mealtimes in students' language development as examinations of family and classroom mealtimes reveal associations between patterns of discourse and students' language gains (Barnes et al., 2020; Beals, 1997, 2001; Weizman & Snow, 2001). Mealtimes may serve to apprentice children into appropriate discourse moves, such as staying on topic, determining the appropriateness of the topic, how to give appropriate amounts of information, and socially acceptable forms of communication (Beals, 1993).

Topics of Conversation

A goal of mealtimes should be to engage your students in interesting conversations that build academic language through discussing topics of mutual interest (see Table 7.1). Consider the topics you enjoy discussing during meals as well as those of your students when developing conversation starters. Certain topics naturally occur in mealtime discussions, such as personal narratives or reminiscing about past and future events, discussion of food, and academic topics such as food and nutrition. Many topics are initiated by students, particularly personal narratives, which naturally makes the topic of interest to the participants (Barnes et al., 2020).

Home-School Connections. Mealtimes can be unique opportunities to make home–school connections and learn about students' lives outside of the classroom. Talking about things that happen outside of the classroom encourages decontextualized talk. Students will need to incorporate more detail and description when talking about events, people, and places that may not be familiar to the other participants in the conversation. This can include rich and varied vocabulary as well as complex syntax.

To spark conversations about students' home lives, you may wish to ask targeted questions. It can be helpful to ask students if they have similar meals at home, how they are prepared, and who prepares them. You may

Table 7.1. Academic Language in Mealtimes

Topic	Language	Teacher Examples/Prompts
Students' Home Lives	Decontextualized talk, rich descriptions and details	"My brother doesn't like vegetables and won't eat them!"
Narratives, Reminiscing	Mental state verbs, sequencing	"Can you tell me about a time that your family prepared a special meal?"
Food	Descriptive language, categorization, scientific vocabulary and topics (nutrition)	"Ricotta cheese is a dairy product that is rich with calcium."
How It's Made	Sequencing, following directions	"After the farmer harvests the tomatoes, they are transported to a processing facility."
Mathematics	Mathematical vocabulary (spatial, quantitative)	"Could you please divide the cake into eight equal slices?"
Culture and Holidays	Diverse vocabulary, argumentation	"Pumpkin pie is my favorite dessert at Thanksgiving because I love putting whipped cream on top!"
Poetry/Song	Figurative language, rich vocabulary, variation in phrases and clauses	"On top of spaghetti All covered with cheese I lost my poor meatball When somebody sneezed"

wish to begin this type of conversation by providing a personal memory or experience where you model the type of responses and language you are hoping to hear from the students. You can share memories of a time you had a similar meal or a memory associated with the food and ask students about their experiences. Reminiscing encourages mental state verb use, (verbs such as *know, think, remember, wish, wonder*) that typically occur in complex syntactic phrases (I remember when my family ate delicious turkey at Thanksgiving). This can be an excellent opportunity to learn more about the students' home lives in addition to discussing cooking and nutrition while nurturing syntactic development.

This is also a time to encourage personal narratives where students share stories or reminisce about events or activities that are not related to the meal or food. Asking students what they did over the weekend, the night before, or at a recent fun experience can often spark exciting conversations. It may be helpful to talk with parents or to send a note home indicating the possible topics that you'll be discussing at mealtimes. This can help caregivers prepare students ahead of the conversation so that each student comes to school feeling ready to share. Keep in mind that not all students will be comfortable talking about their home lives, and that cultural sensitivity should be highly prioritized, hence these discussions should be intermingled with other topics to ensure maximum participation.

Some students may be reluctant to share personal experiences, or may have difficulty with recalling past events, so it may be helpful to talk about events that have recently happened within the classroom. Asking students about a favorite book they have recently read or heard, an activity they enjoyed, or a funny moment can also be excellent options. If you were present for the activity, you can support or scaffold the student's retelling and ask specific questions to prompt memories.

Talk about Food. Knowing the mealtime menu (if available) prior to the meal can be helpful as you can consider how you may engage students in talking about the food that is visibly present. The NGSS include standards focusing on food and nutrition, so mealtimes are excellent opportunities to address some of these standards in a more relaxed atmosphere. Consider discussing the attributes of the food and how it may be categorized (*fruit, vegetable, protein, starch*). For example, when students are eating chicken, you can introduce the term *protein* and explain that it may help to build muscle and repair tissue. Discussion around a "balanced" diet can help students see the benefits of eating a variety of different food types to help fuel their bodies to grow and learn. You may wish to access the resources on the USDA's "Kids' Corner" webpage for additional ideas.

The following conversation occurred during a lunch shared between a small group of students and their teacher in a Head Start prekindergarten classroom. The teacher begins the conversation by posing a question that can be answered by examining the food on the table. The prekindergarten students use precise, academic vocabulary and are casually introduced to fruits, vegetables, and starches. Additionally, the teacher gathers valuable information about what the students already know about fruits and vegetables.

> *Teacher:* Do we have a vegetable today? (*initiation*)
> *Cecilia:* Yeah.
> *Teacher:* What kinda vegetable do we have on our plates? (*extending question*)
> *Xavier:* Banana!
> *Teacher:* Umm. Banana's a fruit. What kinda vegetable do we have? (*clarifying question*)
> *Brynn:* Broccoli!
> *Teacher:* Broccoli and potatoes. Potatoes are something that you call a starch. (*categorizing response*)

This can be a wonderful opportunity to talk about shapes (*rectangle, triangle, cylinder*), textures (*bumpy, smooth, slippery*), flavors (*sweet, bitter, sour*), sizes (*greater than, less than*), quantities or volume (*cup, serving, teaspoon*), or colors (*turquoise, magenta, gold*). Students can also develop arguments for which foods they like the best using complex syntax to express a preference (*I prefer the zucchini because it tastes so fresh*).

Talk About How Food Is Made. A wonderful topic of conversation with younger students can be a discussion about how the food was prepared or where it came from. Asking students how they think more complicated dishes are cooked can reveal and build content knowledge while also promoting components of academic language. Students may try to sequence the task of making a sandwich using ordinal language (*First you slice the bread, then you spread the peanut butter . . .*). You may wish to ask students to identify ingredients in a dish to encourage academic vocabulary and complex syntax.

Students may be asked how the food got to the table. This can include basic discussions of picking garden vegetables, to more complex discussions involving topics such as transportation, refrigeration, and storage. A child may initiate a topic, and you can sustain and elaborate the conversation by posing targeted questions and giving scaffolding prompts that encourage the student to continue talking. Note that other children may join in the conversation and others may simply observe but can still benefit from quiet observation.

> *Sayid:* What's that red thing? (*child initiation*)
> *Teacher:* It is a tomato. (*affirmative response*) Where do tomatoes come from? (*open-ended question*)
> *Sayid:* The kitchen. (*basic response by child who initiated*)
> *Teacher:* Before they come to the kitchen they have to come from somewhere else. (*scaffolding prompt*)
> *Grace:* The ground. (*second child joins*)
> *Dean:* Store. (*third child joins*)
> *Teacher:* The ground. They're grown in the ground. (*affirms answer and adds information*)
> *Sayid:* And you cut it. (*initial child extends discussion of the process*)
> *Teacher:* Yeah, and you can cut them and put them in spaghetti and make ketchup. (*affirms and models elaborated discussion of the topic using complex syntax*)

Discussing Mathematics. Mealtimes may also allow for mathematical discussions that include academic vocabulary. Portion or serving size can be discussed, as well as fractions (*parts* and *wholes*), or quantity. Initially, discussions may focus on developing understanding of the concept (*part and* *whole*), with academic vocabulary included as students are ready (*fraction, half, numerator*). Asking students who ate half of their sandwich or to show you a third of orange can help them to enact key vocabulary terms, which may increase their learning opportunities. Remember to keep the conversation fun and of interest to the students. Do not try to directly teach vocabulary during mealtimes if the students are not interested in learning more about the topic (Hadley et al., 2019).

Culture and Holidays. Many foods are related to specific holidays or cultural events, which may spark conversations rich with diverse and varied vocabulary. For example, students may recognize that pumpkins are related to several fall holidays, which may spark conversations about activities such as carving jack-o'-lanterns or baking pumpkin pies. You may wish to encourage students to talk about times when they have carved pumpkins as an opportunity to utilize decontextualized talk and precise vocabulary. You can encourage younger children to use academic vocabulary such as *carve, scoop, design*, and *select*. Older students also may be encouraged to use these vocabulary terms, but you may wish to focus more on the discourse level by encouraging them to develop an argument for a specific design choice. For example, students can argue for why they prefer scary, artistic, or happy jack-o'-lanterns.

Incorporating Poetry. Poetry is a natural fit for mealtimes due to its brevity, diversity of content, and focus on language. Poetry tends to contain shorter phrases than a traditional book, which may make the content more accessible to younger students or ELLs. It may also repeat words or phrases, which may direct students' attention to them, or may aid with word learning as repetition is key to vocabulary acquisition. Poetry can be a natural way to talk and think about language, and may be especially effective for promoting the oral language development of ELLs (Hadaway et al., 2001).

Poetry may spark conversations about the word, syntactic, and discourse features of academic language. For example, you may wish to discuss how the language in a poem varies based on the needs of the audience as this focuses on the discourse level. Discussing word choices may reflect the lexical level, while discussing sentence/clause/phrase structure reflects the syntactic level. These features may naturally arise when talking with students about what they liked about a poem. Some will naturally discuss the topic, which opens a great opportunity to talk about how the poet uses specific words, phrases/clauses, and tone to discuss the topic. You can also ask students which words or phrases they enjoyed and discuss how the author's use of such words and phrases created a certain mood in the poem. Poetry may also allow for contrasting formal/academic and informal/casual language. Talking about how a poem is similar to or different from a textbook can help students see how different tasks/topics require different types of language.

You may wish to set aside one day per week to share poetry during a meal or snack time. Initially, you may wish to supply the poetry. See Appendix E for online poetry sources. These include both serious and silly poems that can be incorporated into mealtimes, including poetry that is read aloud by the poet. As students become more familiar and comfortable with poetry, you may invite them to share poems of their own creation or those they enjoy outside of school. Parents and caregivers, as well as other faculty members, may be invited to share poetry with your class during a mealtime.

Maintaining the Conversation

Once you have settled on the topic of conversation, it is important to think about how to keep the conversation going. Longer conversations are more likely to develop knowledge and incorporate more diverse and academic language, so consider how you may keep the conversation going.

Mealtimes offer an excellent opportunity to ask real questions to which you do not know the answer. These open-response or open-ended questions can be answered in many ways depending on the experience and knowledge of the respondent. Open-ended questions may be used to start a conversation, "Who can tell me about a time they learned something new?" or may be used to extend a conversation by asking for details or clarification.

Younger children may be excellent conversationalists, but they are still not proficient with providing sufficient details. If they leave something out, make sure to ask them about it. For example, if Jezebel says, "We cooked dinner last night," make sure to ask *who* she cooked dinner with, *what* they cooked, and *how much* everyone enjoyed the meal. These are the types of questions we would ask our friends in a normal conversation, so employ these skills when striving for five conversational turns with younger children. The classic "wh" questions can come in handy: *who, what, when, where, why,* and *how.* If you're not sure what to ask, you can simply request that the child tell you more or say more about their topic, "Can you say more about that, please?" It is perfectly fine to halt the conversation and ask for clarification, "Wait, you did what? Tell me more about that!" Do not pretend to understand what a student is saying; rather, ask questions that inspire the student to add in more detail and descriptions. These questions also show that you value the student's input and may build students' confidence. Make sure to avoid asking too many questions. We do not want students to feel as though they are on a quiz show! Your questions should be driven by natural interest, so when you notice that interest is flagging, make sure to move the conversation on to a new topic.

If you feel a lull in the conversation or cannot think of another question to ask, consider sharing a personal experience related to the topic. If the students have been talking about baking at home, consider adding a short story about your experiences baking at home. Funny stories may be particularly pleasing to younger students. It is perfectly fine to make up stories, too. A fun game can be to tell a story and have the students decide if the story is real or fake and explain their rationale using complex syntax (*I believe your story is true because*, or *Although I enjoyed your story, I do not believe it is true*). This can encourage close listening as students attempt to seek out details that will verify or negate the truthfulness of your tale. Students may engage in a lively debate about the truthfulness of the story!

Make sure to encourage all students to ask questions and share their experiences. Students cannot develop their language abilities without participating, so make sure that everyone has an opportunity to talk (this is also a way to keep conversations fresh). You may wish to incorporate talking tokens (Hadley et al., 2020). Each participant (students and teachers) is provided with an equal number of talking tokens. Each time a person participates in the conversation, that person uses one talking token. When all of that person's tokens are used up, that person must wait until all other participants have used up their talking tokens before having another turn. This visual reminder encourages reluctant students to speak, while also ensuring that more chatty students are not stealing the show.

Conversational Norms

Every family and culture have different ways of talking during mealtimes. It can be important to discuss expectations for mealtime discussions with your students early in the year to develop a culture of discourse norms and facilitate participation. In addition to discussing common rules, manners, and routines, it can also be important to discuss how students should participate in a discussion. You may wish to develop conversational norms with your class as this encourages thinking about language, which may promote metalinguistic awareness.

SHARING TIME

Sharing time, or show-and-tell, is an opportunity for a student to share thoughts, ideas, experiences, or materials with their peers. Sharing time may be an activity that "bridges the gap" between students' home discourse and the academic language of the classroom (Michaels, 1981, p. 423). The teacher may scaffold students' participation in sharing time such that there is a confluence between home and school discourse styles. Because of this,

Michaels (1981) calls sharing time an "oral preparation for literacy" (p. 423). Indeed, studies relate sharing time to the emergence of literate discourse or academic language (Heath, 1983; Peterson & McCabe, 1994).

For sharing time to provide effective support for academic language, students need sufficient time to talk and opportunities for you or students to ask questions or make comments. Limit the number of children who share each day to allow time for each student and to avoid boredom. Some teachers set a schedule so students will know when it will be their turn to share.

There are a variety of formats of sharing time, with each having particular affordances for allowing students to exercise their academic language muscles with adult support and guidance. Many sharing time experiences encourage students to tell a narrative in a sequential order that includes details and decontextualized language to support the audience's understanding. Sharing time may encourage the use of academic vocabulary as students describe experiences and items on which they are experts. As the student is the expert on the topic, a tone conveying this expertise may be incorporated at the discourse level. You can demonstrate value for the various sharing and narrative styles that students bring to the classroom by modeling respectful listening and providing positive feedback on students' contributions.

Sharing time displays offer opportunities for students to practice telling about something that is visually present (such as a favorite object) or an experience that was not shared with their peers, thus encouraging decontextualized talk. Younger students may bring in a favorite object and be asked to explain why the object is special or important. This type of show-and-tell requires the student to develop an argument, which is a form of academic language (*This is my favorite doll because. . . .*). Visual props may help younger children, but there is a risk that having the object will reduce the need for the child to use language to talk about it. Special prompting may be needed to encourage students to talk about things such as where they play with it, and who they play with. Sharing times when students describe events that happened outside of the classroom allow students to tell narratives involving decontextualized language and sequencing, both of which are critical features of academic language.

Modeling Language

You may wish to model many different types of sharing times as you move through the school year. Initially, or with younger children, you may wish to showcase how you present an object of interest, such as a favorite toy, personal keepsake, or treasured object. First, share the object with the students and model a sharing time presentation.

"Today, I brought in my photo album from my family's trip to the Adirondack mountains. We visited many historic sites and saw natural

Table 7.2. Sharing Time Template

Steps	Sample Language
1. Tell the class what you are sharing.	"Today I brought in my . . ."
2. Tell the class why you are sharing this item.	"It's important because . . ."
3. Describe some of the item's history and important features.	"I got it at . . . It was a gift from . . . It reminds me of . . . It's a type of . . . Its special feature is . . ."
4. Open the floor for discussion.	"Does anyone have any questions? What can I tell you more about?"

wonders on our trip. I'm going to show you a few of my favorite photos and explain why I picked them . . ."

After sharing your object, talk to your students about the components of your share. You may wish to provide them with a template for sharing, as shown in Table 7.2.

Other types of sharing time may require different types of models. For example, when asking students to tell a personal narrative, you may wish to read aloud a personal narrative that exemplifies your expectations. Websites such as We Are Teachers or Reading Rockets provide lists of texts that exemplify different types of personal narratives. Many of these may also be useful for writing instruction. Having students first tell their personal narratives during sharing time prior to writing may help students develop more detailed pieces that contain more elements of academic language. It is important to keep in mind that different cultures have different values and ideas regarding narratives. Protacio and Edwards (2015) outline culturally affirming means for engaging ELLs during sharing time, including restructuring sharing time by working with families to plan and prepare their student's share about their native culture.

Materials

Sharing time does not mean that students always need to bring in an item from their home. Purposefully planned sharing times where students are provided with objects or ideas to discuss can be just as fruitful. For example, students may be given a variety of objects and asked to sort them into different categories based on the topic of instruction (fruits, vegetables, shapes, mathematical symbols). Students will then need to name each object (triangle, rectangle), which promotes the use of academic vocabulary. They would then describe each object using its category membership (This shape is a *rectangle* because . . .). Providing specific sentence frames may promote the use of complex syntax as well as potential opportunities for additional academic vocabulary use (it has four *sides* and four *angles*). These details help to form the basis of an argument for why a particular object falls into a certain category. Older students may then engage in writing about their oral displays. This allows them to shift from oral to written academic language and to consider various text features, expand or add details to their ideas, and revise and restate their oral arguments.

Support Strategies

You may wish to incorporate specific scaffolding strategies with a range of supports to facilitate students' engagement in sharing time. Adjusting your prompting of a student should be based on what the student is able to do and the degree of familiarity with the topic or type of discussion.

Gallagher (2016) describes three prompts that may be effectively implemented during sharing time to promote student engagement and use of academic language (see Table 7.3). An *open prompt* provides the least amount of support as it provides limited direction about the expected response. This allows the student to determine the content and form of the response. Open prompts include requests for elaboration or clarification, or metalinguistic explanations (Gallagher, 2016). In contrast, a *directed prompt* specifies the type of response that is desired without scripting the response. This prompt provides more support than an open prompt as it does require a specific answer and is frequently framed in a yes/no or either/or format. Similarly, directed prompts may ask the student to formulate the response in a specific manner. Constrained prompts provide the greatest amount of support as they provide language for students to incorporate within their responses. These prompts may model language by recasting what the student has said in a more grammatically correct or advanced manner or may provide sentence frames that the student can use for formulating a response in academic language.

Table 7.3. Examples of Prompts

Open Prompt	Directed Prompt	Constrained Prompt
When did you go there? How did you arrive at school today?	Would you rather do this or that?	You can start your response by saying, "I believe ___ is the best because . . ."
Please tell me more about . . .	Please tell me in a step-by-step manner. What happened first?	Make sure to include "although" in your response rather than "but."

On the surface, sharing time may appear to be a one-student show, where a single student presents an object or story to a captive audience; however, this need not be the case. Multiple students can participate in sharing time through the incorporation of *questioning, sequencing*, and *developing arguments*. Incorporating audience participation may allow many students to engage in academic discourse and encourage lengthier conversations.

Questioning may help multiple students participate in sharing time. Similar to traditional sharing time, one student takes the stage and begins to present an experience or object: "I went to a party." Other students are then encouraged to ask questions about this initial statement such that additional details are provided using "wh" questions. This can lead to an extended conversation that promotes the use of academic language. These questions may assist the presenting student with the development of a narrative that includes important details (Gallagher, 2016).

Sharing time is also an excellent opportunity to engage students in sequencing events. To support students with sequencing, you can scaffold their abilities by sequencing events known by all participants, such as a recent classroom event. For very young children, sequencing may involve recreating the events of the previous day. Many early childhood classrooms involve a work board or daily schedule that can be a visual aid for supporting this task. Mix up the different activities that were accomplished the previous day and ask students to put them back in order. Once the correct order has been achieved, students can begin to incorporate sequencing language such as *first, next, last, later*. Providing sentence frames may assist with these tasks. Older students may be asked to sequence events in a recently read narrative. Students may work in their reading groups to accomplish this task.

Surprisingly, sharing time can be an excellent opportunity for students to practice crafting an argument, much as one might do in science or social studies. For example, younger students can be asked to bring in their favorite toy and explain why this is their favorite. Using the components of an argument—claim, evidence, rationale (described in Chapters 9 and 10)—the student can build up a clear explanation using their personal knowledge. This can be an excellent way of practicing argumentation based on personal preference rather than world knowledge, thus eliminating some of the cognitive load.

Older students may wish to bring in their favorite books and present an argument about why it is their favorite. Students can be encouraged to use rhetoric to convince others to read their selected book, while also providing a brief summary of the story. This encourages students to incorporate the language of the text and literacy vocabulary (*plot, character, setting*), while also reviewing some of the key plot elements.

CONCLUSION

Informal times may be wonderful opportunities for students to try out different types of academic language in a low-pressure situation. Modeling language, explaining discussion expectations, and encouraging student engagement may help students bridge the gap between home and school language. Providing appropriate support strategies and scaffolds may gently nudge students toward incorporating academic language. Encouraging multiple students to participate in sharing time and mealtime conversation allows for opportunities to practice, while also showing students how to engage in conversation.

CHAPTER 8

Playful Learning

Coauthored by Katherine Newman and Jessica Lawson-Adams

PRIMING QUESTIONS:

1. How can I use drama, music, and games for academic language instruction?
2. What are playful strategies that I can use to teach vocabulary, syntax, and narrative skills?
3. How can I use playful learning methods with 2nd- and 3rd-graders?

Games and music provide excellent opportunities to engage students in activities using and enjoying language in ways that foster academic language development. The activities in this chapter allow you to combine the enjoyment of games with the skill of using language in new ways and the power that accompanies knowledge of new words.

Teachers help students build academic language by providing activities that encourage students to use language for academic purposes. Talk that takes place when students engage in dramatic play and as they sing and discuss the lyrics of songs often leads to conversations about past, future, and imaginary events. Such talk naturally fosters use of complex grammatical forms, use of varied vocabulary, and the construction of imaginary worlds purely with words. Games can also be created that teach academic vocabulary and provide occasions for teachers and students to discuss the meanings of words.

Games and music have many features that enable you to teach words effectively. *Frequent exposure* occurs as activities are enjoyed repeatedly and students are *engaged* and have occasions to use the new words and language structures. Furthermore, music is *multimodal*, as students can sing and move during the instructional activity. We recommend introducing activities with explicit instruction.

DRAMA AND IMAGINATIVE PLAY

Drama and imaginative play activities create an energizing and inclusive space for students to experiment with academic language during activities that are social, imaginative, and involve movement and language. When students plan and act out pretend scenes together, they communicate using more advanced language than they do in everyday conversation (Howe et al., 2005). The language of play often includes (1) advanced vocabulary, (2) longer sentences with complex syntax, and (3) discourse-level features, such as decontextualized talk, which reflects the social function of language used in play. Note how these features are present in the following from a veterinarian office-themed play: "When I come into the office, you say, 'What are your dog's symptoms?'" *Symptom* is a general academic word that it is used across multiple subject areas (Nagy & Townsend, 2012). Also, conceptually rich play themes like vet's or doctor's office encourage students to use clusters of words that are semantically linked such as *bandage, injection,* and *wound* that build networks of knowledge.

Play provides opportunities for students to construct sentences with *complex grammatical forms* as they negotiate scenes and dialogue. The student in the previous example also produced a grammatically complex sentence as they planned the scene with a peer. The sentence contains three clauses and a temporal conjunction (*when*) that sets up a future play action. Teachers can also join the fun as play partners and model grammatically complex talk (Justice et al., 2013). Modeling complex syntax during small-group play may be particularly helpful for ELLs and students with special needs.

The social context of pretend play encourages decontextualized talk because students use language that is not connected to their physical surroundings. Most of the play scenario is unfolding in students' imagination and constructed through language, even when there are props. The student's reference to their play partner's dialogue (you say, "What are your dog's symptoms?") is an example of decontextualized talk because it creates a shared understanding between the players that goes beyond the physical here and now.

Guidelines

Our research with pre-K students found that teacher-guided story reenactments can foster vocabulary development (Dickinson et al., 2019). Storytelling and story-acting also benefit growth of narrative comprehension (Nicolopoulou et al., 2015).

In general, drama and play activities are harder to implement well with large groups, especially with younger students. Small-group time promotes collaboration and greater participation. It also affords the teacher time to respond to individual students and scaffold their language use. The following guidelines will help ensure a focus on academic language:

1. Build on student interests and life experiences. Pretending is a wonderful way to connect students' out-of-school and in-school experiences.

2. Use props that represent key vocabulary and concepts. Select or make props that will spark rich conversation and dialogue during play and link to current themes.
3. Be responsive and follow students' lead. Observe students' play and ask questions that scaffold their language use and learning.
4. Plan for play and drama. Give students opportunities to develop metalinguistic awareness. Model how to collaborate with peers to plan scenes (talk about language).
5. Write about play and drama. Involve younger students in independent writing or dictations of narratives to perform. You may invite older students to compose and perform dramatic pieces such as a character interviews, science documentaries, or historical reenactments from multiple viewpoints. Students may record their enactments and publish them on video-sharing or podcast platforms.
6. Preteach vocabulary. Select words from the play theme that students will use when acting out a role or setting up a scene (see Chapter 4).

Story Reenactment

For students in pre-K and kindergarten, teachers can use books with advanced language and exciting plots as a starting point for imaginative play. Over several repeated read-alouds, you can provide rich explanations of selected words using student-friendly definitions, synonyms, gestures, and an example of the word in a context outside of the story. Following the readings, guide students in small groups through a reenactment using figures and props and encourage use of vocabulary from the story (e.g., Toub et al., 2018). Students can also create craft stick puppets and/or paper plate masks in lieu of figures. Draw attention to words and model complex syntax using these strategies: *narrating* students' play actions ("Look at the knight *charging* fast toward the dragon!"), *commenting on props* that represent focus words ("That *throne* your queen is sitting on is shiny and gold"), and *asking questions* that encourage students to talk about words (How are the dragon's *talons* different from our hands?). After several days of reenacting, encourage students to select a play setting that is different from the story, such as going to the beach or a birthday party, while using the same props and focusing on the same words to encourage creativity and flexibility in use of novel language. Some supervision may be necessary to ensure that all students are participating in the play and to provide support for students less familiar with academic language, such as ELLs.

Storytelling and Story-Acting

Storytelling and story-acting (STSA) gives pre-K through 3rd-grade students the roles of author *and* actor as it draws on students' everyday experiences instead of reenacting a familiar read-aloud. Preschoolers in classrooms that used STSA, originally developed by Vivian Paley, made greater gains in vocabulary knowledge and narratives understanding than preschoolers who did not participate in STSA (Nicolopoulou et al., 2015).

To begin, set up a space during center time for students to compose a story. Encourage students to tell any story. Repeat the student's words as you write them down verbatim, then read the story back to the student. Ask questions like "What happened next?" Prompting students with open-ended questions allows for extended discussion and encourages academic language use. Once the student is finished dictating the story, they select the role they want to enact and select peers for the other roles. The story-acting occurs during group time with all students as the audience. First read the student's story. Then invite all of the student-actors to the "stage" and read the story again as they act out their roles.

STSA is a lively, motivating space in which students hear and produce narratives that reflect their experiences. It scaffolds students' abilities to produce decontextualized language, while also adding in details and descriptive language couched in complex syntax. Older students can write their own stories. They may also revisit their narratives in small group lessons after the enactments, talk about their language choices, and make revisions.

GAMES

There are many reasons teachers should consider finding a place in their classroom for games that foster academic language learning. Games can be especially potent ways of teaching and reinforcing vocabulary while promoting metalinguistic awareness as you discuss words and phrases. Word-learning games can be tailored to match your current classroom theme. As you plan with your team, you can come up with many creative variations on existing games and ideas for new ones.

An especially appealing aspect of games is the potential for students to learn to play on their own. You can first teach a game in a teacher-led group, then support them as they use it in a small group, gradually reducing support as students are able. This provides word-learning opportunities in learning centers to occupy students who have finished assigned work before others. Our discussion here is intended to give you starting points for using games in your room; there are endless methods that you can employ. When you introduce a game, we recommend directly teaching or reviewing words being taught.

Small-Group Games

Teachers can use board games as a means of reviewing words and having conversations about their meanings. These are played with small groups and are especially powerful when a teacher can participate, making corrections as needed, supporting understanding, and encouraging students to use the words. A very attractive feature of teacher-led small-group games is that students listen to each other.

One standard type of board game is the destination game, in which players try to travel from a starting point to a destination. Players may encounter obstacles, setbacks, or sudden changes to move ahead (e.g., ladders, slides, traps, swamps, secret stairways) as they try to reach their goal. You can create your own game board or you can find ways to repurpose boards you find in a thrift store or a yard sale.

For preschool students, we created a simple board game in which students move from a starting point to an ending point traveling along a path (see Figure 8.1). Children pick from a stack of cards that focuses their attention on a target word drawn from the curriculum, which they discuss with the teacher and other children before moving their game piece forward on the path. The key aspect of the game is the conversation about word meanings. The conversation that follows occurred between a teacher and four children playing the game while seated at a table. The teacher holds up a picture card of a child showing his abdomen to begin the conversation.

Figure 8.1. Sample Board Game for Vocabulary Practice

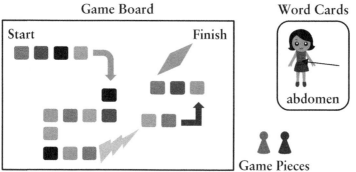

Step 1	Teacher reviews target words
Step 2	Child picks a word card
Step 3	Child and teacher discuss the word meaning
Step 4	Child moves their game piece to the square on the board that matches the border color from their word card (i.e., the child who picks the abdomen card moves their game piece to the next blue square on the board)
Step 5	Next child picks a word card and repeats steps 2–4

Note the teacher's use of "wh" questions to spark conversation and direct student attention.

> *Teacher:* What's this?
> *Lala:* Abdomen.
> *Teacher:* Where it is?
> *(Lala points to her abdomen)*
> *Teacher:* A-a-abdomen (*stretching out first sounds as she looks around at students*). Okay everyone, show me your abdomen (*as she looks around at each of them*).
> *Students:* Abdomen (*while pointing at their abdomens*).
> *Teacher:* (*asking Lala, whose turn it is*) Do you feel hungry or sleepy in your abdomen?
> *Lala:* Hungry!
> *Teacher:* (*speaking to Anthony whose attention had wandered*) Do you feel hungry or sleepy in your abdomen?
> *Anthony:* Hungry.

Large Group Games

Games that can be played with a full group have appeal because all the students have an opportunity to hear, use, and think about the words. For large group games, it is especially important that the teacher reviews the words using word cards before playing the game because you cannot monitor individual students' understanding. They expose students to metalinguistic talk while teaching them basic information about word meanings (see Table 8.1).

MUSIC

Music is an untapped means for teaching students about and with academic language. This medium allows you to connect sounds and words and enables students to learn about other cultures' discourse patterns and historical heritage. Similar to language, music is made up of sound units and often relies on our auditory senses. In language, those sound units consist of words, while in music they are melodic and rhythmic structures. Both music and language require that we actively produce, hear, and process the combination of sounds. Musical activities are fun and engaging. When we hear music, our reward senses are activated and can elicit a positive emotional response (Menon & Levitin, 2005).

The mnemonic power of music can help students encode and retain the language that they hear during musical activities. Studies have shown that having auditory skills in music, such as discriminating between rhythmic patterns, correlates with students' expressive grammar (Gordon et al., 2015)

Table 8.1. Large Group Games for Practicing Academic Vocabulary

Game	Description
Hot Potato	1. Give a student a word card featuring a gesture representing a taught vocabulary term. Students should be seated in a circle.
	2. Start some music. Students pass the card along the circle.
	3. Stop music. The child with the card stands up, says the word represented by the card, and does the gesture. The group mimics the gesture.
Mother May I?	1. Students line up with their picture card at one end of classroom.
	2. The teacher stands at the opposite end of the classroom and says, "If you have the *coop* card, please take three hops forward."
	3. Continue with additional words until one student is able to touch the teacher.
	*As word knowledge grows, begin using more difficult prompts such as, "If you have the card with the small house for chickens, please take two big steps forward." Multiple children can have the same card in order to increase participation during each round.
Swat (Similar to Slap)	1. Show two pictures on an easel.
	2. One student swats one picture with a fly swatter and says the word.
	3. Ask class if student is correct, and encourage all students to repeat the word.
Concentration (Card Game)	Create a set of cards that feature target vocabulary. Your set of cards has pairs that have the same picture. The cards are placed face down and students try to turn over the two that match. Be sure to have students say the word represented by the picture and say something about it.
Card Matching Games (Go Fish)	1. Develop a set of picture cards for target vocabulary, with each term represented twice.
	2. Divide students into small groups. Each student receives seven cards depicting target vocabulary terms.
	3. Students take turns asking the next student in the group if they have a card that matches the one that they are holding.
	4. If the student has the card, they provide it. The receiving student places the matching pair down and both say the word. If the student doesn't have the match, they say "Go Fish" and the asking player draws a card from the pile.
	5. Play moves to the next student until one student has no more cards.
	*For a twist: Ask students for synonyms or antonyms of the target word, use the word in a sentence, or provide a definition.

Game	Description
Bingo	1. Provide students with a bingo board featuring images of target vocabulary terms (rather than numbers).
	2. Draw cards with images of the target terms and have students cover the matching image on their board. The goal is to cover a row or column of images, or the entire board, first.
	3. With the group, discuss the distinguishing features and characteristics of each term as they are drawn.

and phonological awareness (Moritz et al., 2012), and music training may even improve phonological awareness for preschool and kindergarten-aged students (Degé & Schwarzer, 2011; Moreno et al., 2011).

At the discourse level, music may convey information about how people communicate and provide information about different cultures and topics. Additionally, many songs contain lyrical narratives and figurative language. The syntactic features of songs are unique in that they are fine-tuned to fit with the tempo of the song. Songs and chants may include clauses and phrases typical of academic language as they create precise meaning and develop vivid imagery. Music may draw students' attention to specific academic words, phrases, and clauses and emphasize that language is used differently in different settings and contexts.

Music can draw students' attention to language and foster development of metalinguistic awareness. This may help students intentionally think about the words, syntax, and discourse features that they employ in their communication, as well as how authors use language to convey meaning.

Teaching Academic Language with Music

When using music to support language learning in your classroom, it is important to acknowledge the role that music may play in your students' lives. Music can serve to celebrate diverse cultures, thereby fostering self-esteem of those from a culture whose music is used and broadening awareness of that culture for others. Almost every known culture has its own variant of language and music (Patel, 2008). For instance, in the United States, certain parts of Louisiana celebrate Creole language and music traditions. In Mexico and the southwestern region of the United States, Mariachi music and regional varieties of the Spanish language are prevalent among Mexican communities. Leveraging students' home and community knowledge may facilitate access to academic topics and language while also promoting linguistic pluralities and culturally sustaining practice (Paris & Alim, 2014).

Topical Content and Genre at the Discourse Level

Music can reference unfamiliar settings and past events and provide thematic content for units of study. Songs can convey academic content using a rich variety of vocabulary and syntactic and narrative structures.

Topical Content. Music can be an excellent means for teaching academic content aligned with specific disciplines. For example, consider the lyrics from the song "Follow the Drinkin' Gourd." The song is about the Underground Railroad, and a version was sung to secretly inform enslaved people about how to get to freedom. The drinking gourd in the lyrics refers to the constellation of stars known as the Big Dipper. This song can be used to teach lessons around Black history and the Underground Railroad, as well as lessons about astronomy.

Websites such as PBS KIDS and GoNoodle feature songs that cover an array of academic content and involve academic vocabulary and complex syntax. For example, the PBS KIDS program *Nature Cat* features the song "The Beginning of the Stream," which traces the path of water flow while discussing animal and plant life. The contents of the song align with the NGSS standard K-ESS2-2 Earth's Systems. This song contains phrases and clauses (*from the snowy mountain, bears that eat trout*) as well as academic vocabulary (*basking, motion, wandering*). Using such songs to teach content allows for a focus on the words and sentence structures that convey academic information.

Discourse Genres. Some songs are lyrical narratives that tell rich, descriptive stories. For example, the classic Johnny Cash song "Legend of John Henry's Hammer" tells the tale of the African American folk hero who helped build America's railroads, while a Gordon Lightfoot song details the "The Wreck of the Edmund Fitzgerald." These songs convey historical content in narratives while also drawing on linguistic features of different cultures. The narratives employ verses that detail the unfolding story in a manner that is similar to a storybook narrative. Drawing on characters, plot, rising action, and resolutions, these lyrical narratives use music blended with academic content and language.

Similarly, arguments, another academic discourse genre, may be found in protest songs. For example, Woodie Guthrie's "This Land is Your Land," a song commonly taught in elementary schools, makes an argument for equality for all people. The classic Marvin Gaye song "What's Going On" makes an argument against police brutality using academic vocabulary ("escalate," "conquer") and complex syntax. These songs pair meaningful rhetorical devices with moving rhythms to create strong arguments for topics that remain vital today.

Students may enjoy listening to and discussing such lyrical narratives or protest songs or even creating their own. Students may compose and record their own lyrical narratives or arguments/protest songs addressing important historical or current political content. First, listen to the selected song aligned with your unit of study with your students and discuss the incorporated academic language and meaning of the song. You may wish to address how an argument is made or how a narrative is told through mini-lessons addressing these genres. Next, provide students with the lyrics of the song and have them use these lyrics as frames for composing their own songs. You may wish to omit certain words and have students insert their own choices, or have students compose original lyrics that pair with the melodies of existing songs. Providing these frames or sentence stems models complex syntax as well as narrative/argument structure. After students have composed their songs, they should practice singing or chanting their lyrics with the associated melody. This allows them to become more familiar with the academic language involved in their songs. Finally, have students record their songs through the use of available online apps and share their work with appropriate audiences.

Teaching Vocabulary Through Music

Similar to storybooks, music can be a rich source for academic vocabulary. Rhymes, chants, and sound stories can teach academic vocabulary across a variety of disciplines.

Rhymes and Chants. Teachers can use rhymes and chants to introduce students to academic vocabulary. Rhymes and chants are songs that feature no melody or tune, but are rhythmically spoken, similar to a rap. You can use nursery rhymes, poetry, or song lyrics without using the melody. Students often learn the rhythmic pattern and words of rhymes easily, and they are particularly effective in supporting word learning for ELLs.

To use a rhyme or chant, first say it, encouraging students to softly tap the beat on their knees. Repeat the chant, encouraging students to repeat verses after you. Then perform it together, adding percussion instruments or tapping body parts to emphasize beats. To build vocabulary, you can ask students to reflect on the meanings of words and phrases. For example, in the rhyme Jack and Jill, Jack breaks his crown. This is a teaching opportunity about homonyms and the multiple meanings of crown (crown of the head and an ornamental headdress).

Lyrics of the commonly used chant *Cobbler, Cobbler* illustrate how music can enrich students' understanding of academic vocabulary and figurative language.

Cobbler, cobbler, mend my shoe
Have it done by half past two
Half past two is out the door,
Have it done by half past four.

This rhyme focuses on time and uses language to discuss how time is passing. The term *half past two* is mathematical vocabulary, which allows for a rich discussion of telling time on a clock. Additionally, *out the door* is figurative language that may be unfamiliar to students, particularly ELLs, and may require specific instruction. Using this rhyme provides opportunities to introduce academic vocabulary and make cross-curricular connections.

Content-Specific Academic Vocabulary. Music has a set of academic vocabulary terms that are useful not only for music class, but that also provide foundations for ELA instruction. Terms such as *beat, tempo, rhythm*, and *rhyme* are academic vocabulary terms that students may encounter in music instruction to describe musical structure that are also found in ELA instruction with meanings that are similar. For example, very young students will learn about rhyming words in early literacy instruction, while older students may learn about beat and rhythm in a unit of poetry.

Sound Stories. Musicians and composers often use music instead of words to express ideas and emotions. You can draw on this capacity of music to enrich student's learning opportunities during read-alouds by having students represent vocabulary and ideas in a song with sound by creating sound stories (Lawson-Adams & Dickinson, 2020).

To get started, select a text that features academic vocabulary related to your unit of study. Selecting verbs, adverbs, and adjectives may be particularly effective for creating sound stories, as students will be using sound to represent the target academic vocabulary terms. Read through the text and talk with students about the academic vocabulary terms. Explicitly define key words and phrases and then ask them how they might represent that definition through sound. For example, consider the poetry collection, *Gnash, Gnaw, Dinosaur!* (Mitton & Chapman, 2009). *Gnaw* means to chew something with hard, quick bites. Students would need to vocalize a sound and/or find an object or instrument that might make a sound to represent gnawing. They might crumble thick paper quickly or scrape something rough, like a toy, back and forth, quickly on a table. Once students have a sound created, reread the text and have students add the sound effect whenever they hear the word. This positions students to be active storytellers through sound.

Using sound in this manner can highlight nuanced differences in phrases and word meanings. For instance, in *The Pout-Pout Fish* (Diesen & Hanna, 2008), the main fish becomes *astounded* and *aghast* when a new fish gives them a kiss. Both words refer to being shocked and surprised; however, there is a nuanced difference in their meaning. *Astounded* suggests an overwhelming response to the surprise, while *aghast* suggests a degree of horror in one's reaction to the surprise. That element of horror changes what sound would be used for the word *aghast*. Using vocalizations for these words is a great way to characterize the subtle difference in the words. Ask students to sound *aghast* and then sound *astounded*. *Aghast* will have a more harsh, sharp sound of horror or disgust, while *astounded* will have a wowed sound.

This approach to using sound is not limited to just read-alouds. You can also use it in science by, for example, asking students how they might represent the word "photosynthesis" with sound. You can also do a fun version of Guess My Word. After learning several new words, ask small groups of students to create a sound for a target word. Let them perform the sound for the class and then have the class guess which word the sound matches. You can also consider using a soundscape by asking students to retell an entire story pairing sounds with academic vocabulary or phrases. This may be particularly effective for retelling historic events.

CONCLUSION

Through drama and imaginative play, games, and music, you joyfully engage students in learning new words, talking about words, expanding their control of advanced syntax, and gaining facility using and understanding narrative language. We have provided you and your team starting points and are certain that you can fashion methods tailored to your curriculum and the needs of your students. Keep your focus on promoting fun learning activities that build knowledge of the world and language.

CHAPTER 9

Scientific Language

PRIMING QUESTIONS:

1. What makes scientific language distinct from other registers?
2. How can students read, write, and speak like scientists in the classroom?
3. What materials, resources, and engagements can foster use of scientific language?

WHAT IS SCIENTIFIC LANGUAGE?

The language of science is a unique register of academic language that may be quite different from what students have encountered in their daily lives. Not only does scientific language include precise academic vocabulary, complex syntax, and unique discourse features, such as scientific arguments or explanations, but it is also characterized by rich visual displays that convey content, such as tables, charts, infographics, and illustrations.

At the word level, a scientific register is rich with both general and domain-specific vocabulary terms. Scientific language may contain ideas that are abstract or difficult to visualize due to their scale, such as the vastness of the universe or the smallest particles of matter, or the need to observe changes over time, such as a caterpillar becoming a butterfly through metamorphosis. Describing such abstract concepts requires precision of language with abundant technical vocabulary. Scientific language is also laden with morphemes, which are critical for conveying precise meanings. A review of content area words revealed that the following morphemes were exclusively found in science texts: trans, -ism, chem, electro, endo, hydro, micro, -oid, photo, scope, and thermo (Gutlohn & Besselieu, 2014). Knowledge of such morphemes allows for greater understanding of scientific content. Even preschoolers can learn the meaning of hydro- when stopping for a water break at the hydration station.

Scientific language includes specific syntactic features. Rarely are personal pronouns used in scientific language, as the goal is to suppress individual agency or intention and focus instead on causation. Passive voice may be used to foreground causation (*The electrons were excited by the . . .*).

Similar to the academic language of other disciplines, scientific language is informationally dense. This density may be achieved through the inclusion of nominalization, whereby processes are turned into nouns (*evaporation, condensation*). Nominalizations also serve the purpose of eliminating agency (who did it?) and shift the focus to causation (why or how was it done?).

At the discourse level, the language of science is characterized by an expert or authoritarian stance where information is presented as unquestionable fact. This may be conveyed through declarative sentences (*The atmosphere causes stars to appear to twinkle*). Scientists also convey information through lists and rich descriptions.

Scientists also rely on scientific explanations and arguments. Scientific explanations and arguments include a claim, reasoning, and evidence. A claim is an assertion that is derived from evidence, typically achieved through experimentation. The evidence is the data collected during the experiment that supports the claim. The reasoning is the cause for the claim. For example, students can test the power of magnets on a variety of items (metallic and nonmetallic) to explore which items will be attracted to the magnets. After compiling data (evidence) on their experiment (e.g., "the paperclip and metal shavings were attracted to the magnet, but the eraser and rubber duck were not"), they can make a claim that metallic objects were more attracted to the magnet than nonmetallic objects. The reasoning behind their claim would involve a discussion of how the magnets only stuck to metallic objects.

Scientific language is addressed in the CCSS as well as in the NGSS. The CCSS ask elementary students to be able to interpret scientific words in context, write explanatory pieces that are accurate and contain complex ideas, evaluate the scientific reasoning of others using evidence, and be able to share evidence and findings. Similarly, the NGSS embed linguistic expectations in the science and engineering practices strands by asking students to define problems, ask questions, develop explanations, construct arguments supported by evidence, and collect, evaluate, and communicate information. These standards involve academic language that is communicated both orally and in writing, as well as the ability to read printed language and visuals in text to learn new information.

Few students enter school with a strong foundation in the language of science; hence, all students will benefit from modeling and practice with this precise register. Helping students communicate like scientists, through both written and oral discourse, allows for development of conceptual and linguistic knowledge. In order to do so, students should engage in scientific inquiry and investigations where students are positioned as scientists. In this chapter, we describe how to model and encourage scientific language use through incorporating visuals, teaching vocabulary, reading texts, and engaging in inquiry units. We will begin with describing the means for teaching the various components of scientific language and describe how to pull together these components through scientific inquiry units.

TEACHING SCIENTIFIC VOCABULARY

It is important to devote time to teaching general terms that can be used across scientific instruction (*explain, argument, evaluate*), and domain-specific words that are related to specific science domains (*sedimentary, erosion, electron*). General terms can be practiced throughout the course of the school year using the techniques described in Chapter 4, while domain-specific terms can be taught within specific units of study. You may also wish to consider teaching cognates for students who are ELLs (see Appendix E).

Teaching domain-specific terms is important as words are related to concepts and are embedded in domains of knowledge. Indeed, vocabulary is often considered to be a proxy for conceptual knowledge such that deeper knowledge of a topic is related to larger funds of vocabulary knowledge of that topic (Anderson & Freebody, 1981). There is value in teaching vocabulary through taxonomic or conceptual categories (Hadley et al., 2019; Neuman & Kaefer, 2018). Taxonomic categories are groupings of things related to their class. For example, *penguins, falcons,* and *robins* are all birds, which means they share a certain set of features or characteristics. Specifically pointing out these similarities aids with developing broader conceptual understanding that may assist with word *learning*.

To select taxonomically related words, first consider your unit of study and the processes and themes that are central. Using the standards can help with identifying these key words. Make sure to select terms that include a relative balance of nouns, verbs, and descriptive words (adjectives and adverbs), while also considering imageability and concreteness. For example, when discussing changes to Earth's surface, you will want to teach the terms related to processes (verbs and nominalizations) such as *erosion, weathering,* and *deposition*, in addition to nouns that are more imageable and concrete such as *wind, silt,* and *gravel*. More direct instruction may be needed for processes (verbs and nominalizations) than for imageable nouns, which can be taught with images or photos. All of these terms should appear across the texts and materials that you will use for instruction.

Conceptual Word Walls

Word walls can be an excellent option for teaching scientific vocabulary and showcasing the connections between the concepts (Jackson & Durham, 2016). To develop your conceptual word wall, think about how your target terms are connected and the focal scientific process/phenomena. The nature of the relationships should form the basis for your word wall, with each type of relationship having a different representation. The cross-cutting concepts from the NGSS may help with identifying the nature of the relationship. For example, the selected vocabulary terms (*erosion,*

Figure 9.1. Conceptual Word Wall Depicting Target Vocabulary

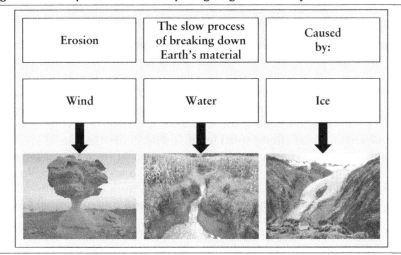

weathering, deposition) can relate to cause and effect processes. Water can create erosion (cause) that results in a canyon (effect). These relationships can be modeled on your word wall (see Figure 9.1). Some relationships may be cause and effect, cyclical, hierarchical, structure/function, webs/concept map, or categorizations. For example, cyclical relationships may be showcased in a circular form with arrows representing the flow or direction of the relationships.

In addition to words and symbols (arrows), you may wish to incorporate other visual aids such as photos or artwork that further exemplify the terms. For example, when discussing weathering due to wind, it may be helpful to show a photo of a rock arch formed by this process. Make sure to label all visuals with the scientific terms. Pairing words with visuals can be particularly helpful for ELLs and students with special needs.

Well-designed word walls can be used for a variety of instructional purposes. Students may use them as organizers for writing projects, such as entries into science journals. Depending on the relationship depicted in the word wall, students may craft arguments or explanations (orally or in writing). You can further support students' use of the word wall by including sentence stems that help students develop language to describe the presented relationships (Jackson & Durham, 2016). For example, stems such as the following may support students' understandings of relationships:

___, _____, and _____ are processes that _____
_____ leads to_____;
_____, _____, and _____ are three examples of _____.

Text Sets

Repetition of target academic vocabulary terms is important for aiding acquisition; hence, students should hear and see these new terms repeatedly. One method for increasing students' exposure to scientific vocabulary is through the use of carefully compiled text sets. Text sets should be comprised of several relatively short texts or articles focused on a specific topic/domain, which contain a set of target vocabulary that is repeated within and across multiple texts. Including a variety of text genres may be beneficial for scaffolding word learning and understanding of scientific content. In particular, younger children may benefit from the inclusion of predictable, narrative, hybrid, and informational texts (Neuman & Wright, 2013). Students who have read or been read to from conceptually-related texts have demonstrated improved vocabulary and content-related knowledge (Cervetti et al., 2016; Pollard-Durodola et al., 2014). The NSTA regularly publishes lists of best STEM books as well as resources for creating text sets.

Vocabulary Game Play

Teaching taxonomically related terms allows for game play! Once students have developed a basic understanding of the target taxonomically related terms, you may wish to have them play a version of the game Guess Who? This game requires participants to ask questions about exclusionary and inclusionary characteristics about a set of pictures in order to guess which picture their competitor has selected. Questions can pertain to the genus or categorization (*Is your animal a mammal?*), differentiating features (*Does your animal have a long snout? Is your animal nocturnal?*). Not only does this fun game help students categorize and differentiate based on characteristics and properties, but it may also encourage students to incorporate precise, academic vocabulary terms (*nocturnal, snout, mammal*).

Morphology can also be incorporated into game play that helps students learn root words, prefixes, and suffixes. Students may engage with morphemes through a word-building activity similar to Making Words (Cunningham & Cunningham, 1992). Rather than build words letter-by-letter, students build words using morphemes (Goodwin et al., 2012). Students may be provided a target base word that reflects the unit of study and be asked to create more words by adding morphemes. For example, students may be given the root word *plant* and asked to make related words such as *planter, planted,* and *implant* (Goodwin et al., 2012). This helps students see the relationships among the words, which may be useful for comprehension.

Scientific Metaphor

Scientific language uses complex syntax to discuss processes and relationships that may be challenging to understand as they are invisible to the naked eye. Many of these "invisible" processes are displayed through scientific metaphor, which uses visual, verbal, gestural, or linguistic components to compare two unrelated things in a manner similar to literary metaphor (Barnes & Oliveira, 2018). Understanding scientific metaphor involves understanding the underlying processes, as well as understanding relational language, which involves complex syntax.

Scientific metaphor is used to map a more concrete and known process to the less familiar or unknown scientific phenomena, such as describing the brain as a computer, sound waves as ocean waves or water ripples, and genes as being selfish. For these language-based examples, the student must understand that *as* is used in a comparative sense to showcase similarities between two different things. Scientific metaphor is also found in visual representations. For example, a visual representation of the life cycle of a frog involves arrows connecting pictures of a frog laying eggs, the eggs hatching into tadpoles, tadpoles developing legs and arms, and finally the tadpole losing its legs to become a frog. When scientific metaphor is presented visually, such as in the tadpole example, students must learn how the symbols or images can be "translated" to words and phrases. For example, the arrows used in a description of a frog's life cycle represent changes over a period of time. Students will need to use phrases and clauses to explain many of these processes that cannot be captured by a single word.

Other scientific metaphors may involve the use of nominalizations, where processes are encapsulated within a single word. For example, a visual display of the water cycle uses nominalization to represent complex processes (water evaporating becomes *evaporation*, falling rain becomes *precipitation*). These visual representations help students to see a process that would be invisible to the naked eye, while also encouraging and supporting the use of complex syntax. You may wish to present a visual aid, such as the water cycle, and have students use complex syntax to describe what is occurring. Sentence stems that focus on the process may be useful. (*Precipitation*) is a process where (*condensation/water/snow falls from the sky*).

Questioning During Read-Alouds

Reading aloud informational texts may help students understand and develop their proficiency with complex syntax. Read-alouds can model syntactically complex scientific language. Additionally, read-alouds are an optimal activity for helping students to pose and answer questions, a critical scientific act, using complex syntax. Questioning can be modeled and scaffolded during read-alouds of informational texts. Explain to your students that scientists ask and try to answer questions. Help students develop a list of questions that can be answered by reading your carefully selected texts. Initially, you may wish to develop a list of questions prior to the read-aloud to model the types of questions that students may wish to pose. Not only does this help students develop questions, but it also helps them see a reason for reading a specific text.

Use the standards to direct students' attention to central themes or processes and help them develop answerable questions. For example, a unit on habitats and adaptations might include the following questions: "What adaptations do certain animals have to help them survive in their habitats?" or "What are the characteristics of an Arctic habitat and the animals who live there?" Frequently, the title of the informational text may help students develop questions. For the text simply titled, *Hibernation* (Kosara, 2012), students may develop "wh" questions: *What is hibernation? Why is hibernation important? Which animals hibernate?* Students may then combine these questions to create greater complexity, which naturally promotes the use of complex syntax: *When does hibernation happen and why does it happen then?* These larger, more syntactically complex questions may span a unit of inquiry or require the reading of a text set to answer.

Materials for Teaching Discourse-Level Features

Scientists use a variety of discourse-level features in their work, such as crafting arguments, explanations, lists, and summaries. Even very young students can practice using these forms of scientific language. The following list describes several discourse-level features of scientific language.

Features and Examples of Scientific Discourse

Language	Example
Predictions	I predict the plastic roof will keep rain off the best.
Recording data	The yellow car traveled 6 feet.
Constructing claims with supporting evidence	The steeper inclined plane will produce faster speeds, as my experiment shows . . .
Making a list	Recording materials for experiment or documenting examples of a particular category (waterproof materials)
Communicating solutions	We used nonstick cooking spray to make the surface slipperier . . .
Summarizing	We blocked the light by using an opaque material . . . This was more effective than . . .

Science Journals. Science journals are a particularly effective means for teaching about and with discourse-level features of scientific language. When students write in science journals, they should be taught several forms of writing that are useful to scientists. For example, scientists make lists, particularly when they are conducting an experiment. A good scientist will list all of their materials as a record. As you engage in scientific inquiry, you may wish to have students develop a list of the required materials or to record a list of steps that were used to complete an experiment (see Figure 6.3 for an example). Students may also be asked to summarize, describe, explain, or craft an argument in their science journals. Students may create charts and graphs to represent their data. Each of these constitutes a form of academic language.

It is important to first model each of these features and explicitly demonstrate how a discourse-level feature is used and developed before asking students to work independently. Providing sentence stems such as "I think ___ will happen because," or "I believe the ___ will be faster than the ___ because" can help students to make predictions as well as support their assertions. Providing templates may facilitate list development, while graphic organizers may be used for crafting arguments or creating summaries (see Appendix E).

Remember that science journals need not be constrained to paper and pencil. Journals may be created through online platforms such as Prezi, VoiceThread, Jamboard, Seesaw, or Google Slides that allow students to use audio, text, and visual to convey meaning. These multimedia displays can be shared virtually among students as well as with the teacher, particularly through platforms such as Google Classroom. Incorporating technology allows all students to access the curriculum and may provide additional support for students with special needs or those who are learning English.

Incorporating Visuals. A key component to science is observation and documentation; therefore, it can be helpful to carefully consider how materials, such as visual aids, may be useful. Younger students may benefit from the use of digital photography for capturing scientific phenomena and positioning them to observe and record like scientists (Britsch, 2019). The photos serve as anchors for the discussions as students have a clear visual aid from which to draw their observations. For example, students can discuss how the size and frequency of bubbles change when observing water reach its boiling point. Photos may help to capture these changes and allow students to compare and contrast these differences over time. Placing the images side-by-side can help students to see the differences, which can then be described orally or in writing using scientific language.

Students may wish to label their digital images using target vocabulary terms through the use of editing or presentation software. For example, students may capture images of flowers and trees and be asked to label the various parts using target vocabulary terms from the unit of study (*pistil, stamen, petal, stem*). Students may then compare and contrast their images to observe how they are similar or different from those captured by their peers (e.g., My flower had six petals while Juan's flower only had three). These comparisons may form the basis of a science journal entry that is rich with complex syntax and academic vocabulary.

PULLING IT ALL TOGETHER

Science is based on inquiry because scientists pose questions that are answered through experiments. As children are naturally curious, engaging in experiments to answer the common questions of "Why?" or "How?" creates motivation to uncover scientific principles and concepts while engaging with academic language. It may be helpful to consider using inquiry units or project-based learning that focuses on specific themes, cross-cutting ideas, or strands in science as outlined in the NGSS. Academic language can be woven into these strands, particularly when students are encouraged to engage in scientific experiments, observations, and engagements.

The following section describes a scientific unit aligned with the standards that would be appropriate for instruction in a pre-K or early elementary classroom. Units such as these blend together science and ELA standards as students learn scientific content through reading, writing, speaking, and listening. We focus on the academic language modeling and instruction rather than the scientific content. For more information about the scientific content, please review a full unit description published in *Science and Children* by Lemaster and Willet (2019).

This unit of study investigates *pushes* and *pulls* while discussing force and motion. It builds from the Touch, Talk, Text model (Carrier et al., 2020), which advocates for using scientific experiments, discussions, and read-alouds for building scientific language. *Touch* involves engaging students in hands-on experimentation relating to the topic of study. Students may also observe videos of others completing the experiment if appropriate. *Talk* refers to having students verbalize the science processes occurring in the experiment. They should be encouraged to include precise scientific vocabulary and complex syntax to demonstrate relationships such as cause and effect. *Text* refers to incorporating informational texts that further demonstrate and explain the scientific phenomenon under study. You may also wish to encourage students to produce texts such as science journals, lab reports, tables, or charts. In this unit, students are primed to discuss the target concept by watching a video on pushes and pulls prior to any formal instruction. Students should be asked to carefully observe what is happening in the video so that they may discuss what they see later.

During the discussion following the video, you should record the key vocabulary terms that students use on a Words We Know chart. This priming activity begins to get students thinking about the topic while also serving as a vocabulary assessment. A second chart, Words We Are Learning, should also be displayed to showcase the target vocabulary that will be focused on during instruction. You can then begin to introduce the preselected target vocabulary terms not yet known to the students through reading informational texts from a predetermined text set. As students begin to use the target vocabulary in their speaking and writing, move the term from the Words We Are Learning list to the Words We Know list. As you continue through the unit, develop a conceptual word wall with the target terms to represent how they are related.

As you read through your texts, engage students in demonstrations and experiments where they are tasked with testing and exploring the concept under investigation. For example, in a unit on pushes and pulls, students can use playground equipment to see how different forces produce different types of motion. Students should craft predictions, record observations/data, create summaries, and present findings in their science journals and lab reports using scientific language. Incorporating visual aids and graphic organizers can be helpful for scaffolding scientific language. Venn diagrams are useful for comparing and contrasting (e.g., similarities and differences between pushes and pulls) and tables and charts are helpful for documenting differences in numerical data (e.g., how adjusting the force applied to a ball relates to the height it bounces) or organizing specific data to the task at hand. Having students work in pairs or small groups and encouraging them to discuss their observations and collected data prior to completing the graphic organizers encourages scientific talk.

Students may wish to compose a story about their explorations (e.g., developing a narrative about balls bouncing to demonstrate motion) or draw or capture digital images, which can be labeled with target vocabulary terms. Older students may be able to develop scientific metaphors to describe unseen processes (the arc of a swing is a smile). Each of these activities serve to build students' understanding of scientific content as well as foster scientific language use. You may wish to promote more scientific talk through purposeful prompts, such as "Can you think of another way or another solution?" or, "That is an interesting idea; does anyone else have another idea, or can they build off of what Sheila said?" can encourage increased dialogue that incorporates scientific language.

CONCLUSION

The language of science takes many forms and includes technical terms, dense syntax, and specific discourse features. Students who understand this register can talk and write like scientists as they convey their scientific knowledge. Engaging students in activities and experiments that promote conceptual development also serves the purpose of increasing students' opportunities to hear and use scientific language. Science instruction should be viewed as a rich opportunity for enactment. Positioning students as scientists encourages them to inquire deeply, pose and explore questions, and convey findings. Each of these activities have scientific language at their core, hence integrating academic language instruction into science engagements can be seamless.

CHAPTER 10

Mathematical Language

PRIMING QUESTIONS:

1. How do you encourage classroom discourse in your mathematics instruction?
2. What materials can be incorporated to help students craft mathematical arguments and explanations? What supports can be provided to help students develop claims, evidence, and reasoning?
3. How can you incorporate mathematical vocabulary instruction across the day? What activities, materials, and engagements can you utilize to promote mathematical vocabulary use?

WHAT IS MATHEMATICAL LANGUAGE?

Mathematics is rooted in language. Language influences how students develop meaning and conceptual understanding of processes and symbolic representations. Indeed, research links difficulties with language rather than numerical processing with mathematical difficulties (Vukovic & Lesaux, 2013). Mathematical facts are stored in language-specific ways, which can impact students' symbolic representation and problem-solving methods.

Mathematical language is more important than ever due to the recent shift from rote memorization to solving word problems deeply rooted in language. Indeed, four of the eight Effective Mathematics Teaching Practices from the National Council of Teachers of Mathematics (NCTM) focus specifically on language: questioning, discussing, and evaluating student understanding through discourse (NCTM, 2014, p.10).

Mathematics has a distinct academic register that is characterized by symbolic notation, visual and graphic displays, technical vocabulary, conjunctions with technical meanings, implicit logical relationships, dense noun phrases, and *being* and *having* verbs that connote specific mathematical functions. A mathematical register is very precise, due primarily to the fact that mathematics relies on measurement and calculation.

At the lexical level, mathematics vocabulary tends to have meanings specific to mathematics to develop precision (Schleppegrell, 2007). It has many terms that may seem familiar to students, such as *table, scale,* and *range,* but they have specialized meanings when used to talk about mathematics. A table, for example, in mathematics refers to a visual representation, not the table one eats at during meals. Additionally, words such as *and* sometimes refer to specific mathematical functions. Consider how two and seven equals nine, where *and* refers to addition. Such words are called *polysemous* and can be tricky because students think they understand their meanings, when they actually have new meanings when part of mathematical discourse.

Sentence-level features of mathematical language may diverge from casual conversation, particularly in the ways syntax and cohesive devices are used (or not). The language of mathematics contains many noun phrases to create precision (*right angle, the hypotenuse of the triangle, the area of a polygon*). Students may need support to understand how these groups of words work together to create meaning. Additionally, mathematics contains complex sentences with connecting words and conjunctions between clauses (*but, and, or*). These lengthy sentences add precision but may be challenging for younger students due to the density of information.

At the discourse level, students will need to understand mathematical argumentation and be able to engage in discussions using a mathematical register. The CCSS (2010) note that students should be able to construct and articulate mathematical arguments using formal language and complete linguistically complex tasks that go beyond rote memorization.

MODELING MATHEMATICAL LANGUAGE THROUGH READ-ALOUDS

Teachers may serve as models for using mathematic language because students' growth in mathematical knowledge is associated with adults' use of mathematical language (Purpura et al., 2017). Many young students will likely have had limited exposure to mathematical language and also will lack the reading capabilities to access mathematical language in print (Riccomini et al., 2015). As a result, classroom instruction that draws students into conversations that require understanding and use of this language is important.

One method for modeling mathematical talk is through shared book reading, or dialogic reading, where a teacher and students engage in reading and discussing a storybook. Students' mathematical abilities have been associated with adult–student talk during shared book reading (Barnes & Puccioni, 2017), as well as knowledge of mathematical language (Hassinger-Das et al., 2015; Purpura et al., 2017). Many storybooks and informational texts contain mathematical language pertaining to spatial (*before, near, after*), quantitative (*more, less*), and comparative (*combine, take-away*) relationships.

When selecting texts to expose students to a mathematical register, make sure to focus on selecting texts that emphasize mathematical language. It may be helpful to first identify the mathematical language that you will be targeting in your instruction and then select a text that features such language. Some textbook series provide suggestions for books that convey mathematical language. Websites such as the Math Forum from the NCTM and Book Finder on Reading Rockets may also provide a wealth of suggestions (see Appendix E). Table 10.1 lists some helpful texts you may wish to explore.

Table 10.1. Storybooks Featuring Mathematical Language

Title and Author	Mathematical Language
Two Greedy Bears, Ginsburg (1998)	Divide, equal, part, whole, piece, bigger, smaller, half
Caps for Sale, Slobodkina (1940)	With, without, same, short, long, bigger, smaller, add, subtract
Harold and the Purple Crayon, Johnson (1955)	Straight, short, long, none, more than, less than, left over
Olivia, Falconer (2000)	Enough, before, after, closer to, add, subtract
Mike Mulligan and His Steam Shovel, Burton (1939)	Some, as many as, least, greatest, part, whole, add, subtract
The Snowy Day, Keats (1962)	Equal, before, after, add, subtract, more, less, pair
Albert's Bigger Than Big Idea, May (2013)	A lot, away, below, bigger, biggest, few, high, higher, inside, middle, more, most, near, on, on top, outside, smallest, too big, up
Little White Rabbit, Henkes (2011)	A lot, above, away, below, between, big, bigger, bottom, closer, far, farther, few, many, more, near, over, same, small, smaller, through, top, under
Many Is How Many? Podendorf (1970)	A lot, behind, far, big, few, fewer, fewest, in front of, longer, more, most, near, over, smaller, under
Albert Is Not Scared, May (2013)	A lot, away, around, back, down, more, farther, few, fewest, fewer, first, front, in, inside, last, near, out of, outside, short, tall, top, toward, under, up
Just Enough Carrots, Murphy (1997)	A lot, any, enough, far, few, fewer, fewest, in, inside, many, most, more, near, out, outside, same, too many
Rosie's Walk, Hutchins (1967)	A lot, above, around, behind, below, beneath, between, bottom, down, few, higher, highest, in, in front of, inside, lowest, many, near, on, over, through, toward, under

Source: Adapted from Purpura et al. (2017) and Hassinger-Das et al. (2015).

When necessary, you may need to provide examples that further clarify the language. Using the illustrations and surrounding text for further developing meaning can be an excellent strategy for contextualizing the language (*The illustration shows Janie dividing up her 15 marbles into three equal groups of five*). Reviewing the meaning of the language after the read-aloud may also help with acquisition and retention.

You may also wish to incorporate mathematical language into your discussion even when it is not directly written in the text. Asking questions about the pictures (*Are there more cupcakes or cookies on the plate?*), or discussing the images (*It looks like the bird is flying above the airplane!*) can be additional opportunities to incorporate mathematical language.

TEACHING MATHEMATICAL VOCABULARY

When teaching mathematical vocabulary, carefully speak the word aloud, spell the term, illustrate the term visually, and use it in mathematical discourse. Additionally, encourage students to compare and contrast similar terms (synonyms and antonyms) using examples and nonexamples, and study word parts and morphology. Students receiving instruction involving a combination of these strategies showed growth in mathematics knowledge and vocabulary (Firmender et al., 2014).

As with general academic vocabulary instruction, the amount of support for teaching words may depend on the difficulty of the term. Orosco (2014) developed a four-tier system for categorizing mathematical vocabulary, as shown in Table 10.2. Basic and intermediate terms may require less direct instruction than advanced-intermediate and technical terms. Make sure to also consider how concrete or imageable the term is.

Table 10.2. Level of Difficulty of Mathematics Terms

Level	Description	Examples
1. Basic	Terms commonly heard in everyday talk	Before, after, together
2. Intermediate	Terms that are mathematical in nature and that span mathematical content areas	Addition, digits, division, solution
3. Advanced-Intermediate	Mathematical terms that are only associated with a specific mathematics content area	Denominator, divisor, quotient
4. Technical	Technical vocabulary associated with a single mathematical topic	Perimeter, hypotenuse, vertex

Figure 10.1. Example of a Mathematics Dictionary Card

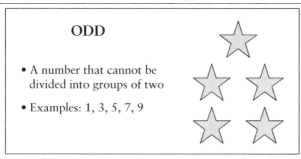

ODD

- A number that cannot be divided into groups of two
- Examples: 1, 3, 5, 7, 9

Mathematics Dictionaries

As many of these terms are not heard in casual conversation, and have meanings that differ from casual use, it may be helpful for students to create a mathematics dictionary. Each target term can be written on an index card (see Figure 10.1). This allows students to practice spelling the term. Students should write a description of the term on the back, and if appropriate, draw a visual representation of the term. If the term is associated with a symbol (such as equals) or a representation (such as a graph), have the students include the symbol or representation on the back of the card as well. Students should note if there is a root word, prefix, or affix that helps with better understanding the term (*octo, poly, tri.*). These cards can be attached to a jump ring, which can be clipped onto a binder or stored with the student's belongings.

Helping students craft definitions of mathematical terms may aid in their acquisition and understanding. In particular, dictionary-style definitions are helpful in a mathematical context as they categorize and provide differentiating characteristics for the term (*a parallelogram is a quadrilateral that has two sets of parallel sides that are equal in length*). The inclusion of such categorizations helps students understand the technical relationships among concepts, distinguish important and exclusionary features, or demonstrate the function of the term. All of these features aid in vocabulary acquisition.

These mathematics dictionaries can be used during mathematics lessons as well as during transition times. For example, students can work in groups to cluster a specified set of cards to discuss the relationships between the terms (Riccomini et al., 2015). This may help students pay attention to the particular attributes of each term and notice similarities and differences. Additionally, these cards can be useful for transition times. Students may play vocabulary line frog (Riccomini et al., 2015) when transitioning between classrooms. The student at the end of the line may be asked to provide a definition or example of a key term from the mathematics dictionary. If correct, the student can jump to the front of the line. Students may also be asked to match a key term to a provided definition or to appropriately use the key term in a sentence such that understanding of the meaning is clear. You may wish to allow multiple students to respond, or allow for many rounds, to increase student engagement.

Decision Trees

Creating or using decisionmaking trees for mathematical vocabulary can help students align distinguishing features of class membership, which is helpful for developing depth and breadth of understanding (see Figure 10.2). Decision trees ask a series of questions that "branch" out into possible choices. As the user moves through the branches, the number of choices or options is reduced until a final decision is made. Decision trees start with a single box (root) that represents the overarching concept. The branches that spring from the root describe different features or properties that may be possessed by different groups or items that fall under the overarching concept. This sorting allows students to see similarities and differences among the mathematical terms.

For example, a decision tree could be used to sort geometric shapes (concept) and show the relationships among them (class membership). This activity aligns with the standard CCSS.Math.Content.KG.B.4, which asks students to analyze and compare shapes to describe similarities, differences, parts, and other attributes. Students should be provided with a list of geometric shapes that they are seeking to distinguish (*parallelogram, trapezoid, circle, oval*). It may be helpful to pair illustrations or visuals of the shapes along with the

Figure 10.2. Portion of a Decisionmaking Tree for Sorting Mathematical Vocabulary

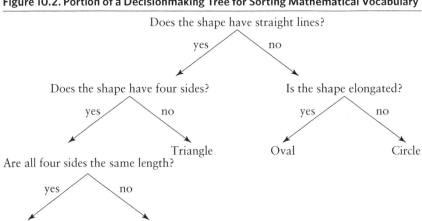

printed vocabulary term. Students should select a shape to identify and follow the flow chart of questions that ask about differentiating characteristics such as whether the shape is composed of straight or curved lines.

Following along the decision tree will help students narrow down their choices and see how each shape is unique and fits into a particular class. At the conclusion of the activity, students will have sufficient information to provide or create a comprehensive definition for each shape (*A trapezoid is a shape with four sides and angles, and only one pair of parallel sides*). Starting with the root (shape), students can follow along the branches to include descriptive features that are unique to the target vocabulary term and help to distinguish it from other members of the class. Older students may enjoy creating their own decisionmaking trees. Students can also play a Guess My Shape game in a manner similar to Guess Who? In this game, students ask each other yes/no questions to see if they can determine the shape selected by the other student.

MATHEMATICAL DISCOURSE

At the discourse level, mathematical language relies heavily on explanations and arguments for showcasing students' understandings. Many standards ask students to provide a rationale for their choices, as well as require the ability to develop arguments based on evidence and examples. Additionally, students may be asked to provide oral explanations of visual representations and read information presented in word problems. Mathematical language may be contextualized (count the number of teddy bears) or decontextualized such as the language used in word problems (*Seven people are traveling to Minneapolis on a train leaving at 9:30 A.M. . . .*). Importantly, students will need to take an expert stance using a formal tone to convey their mathematical understanding. This includes talking like a mathematician.

Creating a Classroom Discourse Community

Mathematical conversations in your classroom allow students to display their thinking while exercising their language skills. Indeed, teachers are encouraged to create meaningful mathematical discourse (NCTM, 2014, p. 29). Developing routines for mathematical discussions may facilitate the creation of a classroom discourse community where students are encouraged to share their thinking in a safe, respectful environment. Discussions also encourage students to fully engage their listening skills, which allows them to observe other students' mathematical language in use.

You may wish to utilize mathematical discourse when beginning new units of study or introducing new concepts or processes. To begin, select an authentic problem that can be addressed through the instruction provided in the upcoming unit. For example, in a unit on measurement you may ask students to measure a space in the classroom so they can help determine the size of a new bookshelf to be ordered. Ask the students to develop a solution to the problem individually or in groups using provided tools (paper/pencil, manipulatives, rulers). Each group or individual should develop one method for solving the problem and prepare to share their idea with the class that includes their rationale. Younger students may benefit from sentence stems for developing their responses (*I selected image number* ___ *because*____. *We think you should add the first* ___*and then* _____). All students may benefit from having a word bank to access for technical terms they may wish to use in their responses.

Steps for Creating a Classroom Discourse Community Through Authentic Problem Solving

Step 1: Select an authentic problem to be solved based on the content of the current unit.

Step 2: Have students attempt solutions to the problem individually or in small groups. Provide appropriate tools for helping students enact the solution (such as a ruler, paper, or manipulatives).

Step 3: Have students present their best solution to the class orally or in writing. Provide sentence stems as needed. Record solutions for public viewing.

Step 4: Engage the class in a discussion about which solution seems to be the best option for the problem. Help students develop an argument for why one solution is best.

Students can be encouraged to discuss why they agree or disagree with other solutions (*I agree with Rashid's solution because. . . . I respectfully disagree with Maudie and think . . . because . . .*), which allows them to practice using mathematical vocabulary couched in complex syntax. It can be useful to develop a classroom list of possible solutions. Publicly displaying student thinking allows others to witness the variety of solutions as well as hear the language of others as they present their thinking. Prior to engaging in such activities, it is important to establish classroom discourse norms, as described in Chapter 6.

Revoicing and Restating

Publicly sharing responses also allows for revoicing and recasting casual language into a more mathematical tone. Revoicing involves clarifying or extending students' language, which is a practice that may be particularly effective for ELLs and younger learners. For example, when solving a word problem about dividing three ice cream bars between six people, a student might respond by suggesting, "We can cut the bars into two pieces." The teacher then can re-voice the good suggestion into, "Great idea! We can divide each ice cream bar in half!" Note how the teacher acknowledged the mathematical thinking in the response first and then incorporated mathematical vocabulary to clarify the response. Students may also be prompted to revoice their own responses, or those of a peer, into mathematical language. You can carefully and sensitively scaffold this interaction by asking students to think about how a mathematician might respond or asking students to talk like mathematicians.

Similarly, students and teachers can restate presented ideas as a means for clarifying and creating greater precision during mathematical discussions. For example, note how the teacher restates and expands on the student's response:

> *Student:* I cut up each bar into two pieces so everybody could have one.
> *Teacher:* So, what I'm hearing you say is that you cut up each bar into two pieces so each person can have one. Do you mean that when you divided the three bars into two pieces, you created six equal pieces so the ice cream bars could be equally shared between six people by giving each person one piece? (restates and expands).

For students who are more linguistically and mathematically adept, the teacher may simply restate the original solution and allow the student to add additional details. This can also be prompted by saying, "Please tell me more."

Arguments

Discussions are also an excellent time for students to practice making mathematical arguments or explanations using mathematical language. Here, we define mathematical arguments as a form of academic communication where students try to convince others of a specific claim through the use of reasoning and evidence, as described in the CCSS. Students may be able to create oral arguments that include a claim and support when they are 5 years old (Macedo, 2011), with their abilities to do so in writing developing later.

To craft an argument, students should begin by developing a claim, which is usually a solution or proposed solution to a problem (see Figure 10.3). Next, students should support their claims by explaining their reasoning. This reasoning may be the steps that they took to solve the problem. Additionally, students may need to provide evidence or examples to further support their claim. This may include showing how the solution or approach to solving the problem can apply to other situations.

Explicitly teaching the format of a mathematical argument can help all students successfully demonstrate their understanding. Encouraging younger students, ELLs, or students with special needs to present their information

Figure 10.3. Features of a Mathematical Argument

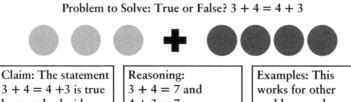

Problem to Solve: True or False? 3 + 4 = 4 + 3

Claim: The statement $3 + 4 = 4 + 3$ is true because both sides equal 7.	Reasoning: $3 + 4 = 7$ and $4 + 3 = 7$	Examples: This works for other problems such as $5 + 1 = 1 + 5$.

through multiple modalities may be useful. For example, students may present their claims orally and then use illustrations or manipulatives such as blocks, counters, or drawings to demonstrate their rationale and provide examples.

When teaching mathematical argumentation, it is useful to first provide students with an authentic problem to solve. Younger students may engage in physical tasks (such as measuring a piece of classroom furniture with strips of paper), that allows them to act out the mathematical processes. The solutions students develop for these questions become the claim in the argument. You may wish to provide sentence stems that model a variety of claims for students to use (*I believe* ___ *because. We found the answer to* ___ *by doing* _____. *The statement is true/false because* _____).

By enacting the mathematical function, students are creating evidence for their claims. You may wish to capture their evidence through photographs or have students orally present their solutions to the group. They may use these enactments to create rationale to support their arguments. Rationale is frequently given in a step-by-step fashion, so helping students to sequentially organize their enactments may be helpful.

> First, we laid out our strips of paper end-to-end. We made sure that none of the edges overlapped. Next, we counted up all of the strips of paper. Finally, we recorded our answer.

Creating public displays of students' arguments that include the claim, evidence, and rationale provides a model of mathematical language and problem solving for future reference.

Materials

It can be helpful to think about how specific materials can lead to mathematical discussion, particularly those materials that may allow students to argue for their position or to explain their thinking. Newell and Orton (2018) discuss activities such as "Number-Talk Images," "Which One

Doesn't Belong," and "Estimation 180" for promoting mathematical discourse. In each activity, students are presented with images and asked to make mathematical assertions that they are able to support using mathematical language (see Appendix E). Activities such as these may easily be transitioned to online learning though platforms, such as Google Meet or Zoom, or asynchronous sharing tools, such as VoiceThread or ChatterPix.

CONCLUSION

The language of mathematics is rich with technical vocabulary and complex syntax. Intentional use of instructional techniques such as read-alouds, direct instruction of vocabulary, and facilitation of discourse communities may help students transition from casual to mathematical language. Modeling language and providing students with multiple opportunities to practice lays a foundation for conceptual development. Make sure to be explicit and provide adequate support for students as they engage in newer forms of language use that are specific to this discipline. Highlighting the links between visuals and language, while also noting the differences among word meanings across disciplines, can help students appreciate the precision that mathematical language can convey.

Assessment

Just like other areas of classroom instruction, academic language requires attention through assessment to inform and improve instruction, differentiate based on individual students' needs, and examine student growth over time. While an emerging field of study, teachers can assess their students' academic language skills and can self-assess their classroom support for academic language development.

PRINCIPLES OF LANGUAGE ASSESSMENT

There are several important principles to keep in mind when assessing student language, including academic language. Language is used in every social context and for a variety of purposes. Thus, academic language assessments should take into account student identity, context, and the levels of academic language.

Assessment should be as *authentic* as possible. For example, carefully observing students engaging in academic discussions with their peers is an ideal way to evaluate the students' use of academic vocabulary, syntax, and discourse with classroom supports (peer conversation partners as well as talk structures and routines, sentence frames, anchor charts, and so on). Likewise, having an individual conversation with a student about an academic topic, such as a book discussion or a writing conference, provides valuable insight into their academic language usage with varying levels of teacher scaffolding. Written artifacts produced as students engage in a variety of academic tasks provide another lens for assessment.

Another important consideration is the distinction between a *difference* and a *deficit*. Often, we hear headlines about the "30 million–word gap" and teachers lamenting that a student, "came to school with no language." In fact, all students have language strengths and knowledge from their experiences in their families and communities. When you approach assessing students' use of academic language, you should consider the linguistic diversity of your classroom, including students who speak a variety of dialects and students who are bilingual or multilingual. Narratives are an example of an area of academic language that is strongly influenced by students' backgrounds and experiences. It is well-documented that children from varied backgrounds use different narrative styles during "sharing time" (Cazden, 2001; Michaels, 1981). In assessing a student's narrative discourse, you can focus on recognizing the different narrative skills your students bring to the classroom to then identify new academic narrative styles to add to their toolbox. By pinpointing your students' linguistic strengths and abilities, you can build upon them.

In addition to the differences between students in terms of academic language, you should also consider the differences within an individual student as they use language in different contexts and for different purposes. The language of schooling has certain "rules," and as educators, we ask students to perform in certain ways with language. However, children do not always display their full range of academic language capabilities in an individual performance in a single setting. This is the important principle of *competence* versus *performance*. A student may be competent in using complex syntax to explain their ideas, but they may not perform that syntax use in a mathematics discussion. The same student may contribute frequently with their syntactic abilities on full display during a discussion of a book they love. Likewise, some students may perform very differently on an assessment of written language as compared to oral language. Due to affect, motivation, language background, or print literacy skills (particularly for emergent readers and writers), these different modes may yield very different results. For example, a student's performance on a written assessment of academic vocabulary may be limited by their word reading or fine motor skills, while an oral assessment would more accurately reflect their competence using academic language. It is recommended that your assessment of student academic language incorporates information from a variety of settings and both oral and written tasks. As language use and development is dynamic in the early childhood years, you should also monitor student progress in academic language use by observing and assessing over time to recognize student growth.

Finally, assessments must be *realistic* for you as the teacher. Assessment plans or systems that require frequent or lengthy individualized administration, or standardized assessments that require young students to work independently for long periods of time, are not realistic when instructional time is so precious at this critical period in a child's education. We keep these principles in mind as we recommend ways of assessing academic language in your classroom.

INFORMAL ASSESSMENTS

Informal assessment is necessary to capture students' authentic academic language use and their full range of competence with academic language.

Observing

One of the most powerful tools for informal assessment of oral language is observation. You should strive to observe all of your students' language use throughout the day and in a variety of settings. Ask yourself the following questions to guide observation in the classroom. If you can't answer each of these, you may need to collect more data!

- What types of academic vocabulary does the student use?
- How long and how complex are the student's sentences?
- Which discourse functions (e.g., questions and answers, explanations, cause and effect, compare and contrast, narrating, presenting) does the student use?
- How does the student's use of academic language vary between grouping structures (e.g., one-on-one with the teacher, one-on-one with peers, in small groups, in whole-class discussions)?
- How does the student's use of academic language vary between activities or content areas (e.g., literacy, math, science, art)?

Keep it simple; open-ended anecdotal notes or a checklist can guide your observation. A checklist developed for preschool children and found to be effective in identifying children at risk of language development problems is the Teacher Rating of Oral Language and Literacy (Dickinson et al., 2003). Table 11.1 is a simple checklist for observing student language in the classroom. It may be helpful to engage a colleague (such as an instructional assistant, speech-language pathologist, student teacher, or literacy coach) to help you with observational data collection.

You may also look more carefully at discipline-specific academic language use in various settings and registers as described in earlier chapters. For example, you might observe students' use of mathematical or scientific academic language practices. Appendix B also provides observational tools for this purpose. Students' names, along with the dates of the observations, may be placed in the top row. The subsequent rows list behaviors associated

Table 11.1 Academic Language Checklist

Student name: Setting: Date:	
Speaking: ☐ Contributes to discussions ☐ Uses precise academic vocabulary when appropriate to communicate ideas ☐ Asks questions ☐ Answers questions ☐ Supports ideas with evidence ☐ Uses language to accomplish academic tasks (e.g., summarize, argue, explain, retell) **Listening:** ☐ Listens actively to teachers and peers ☐ Demonstrates comprehension of information and directions	**Academic words and phrases used:** **Observations and notes:**

with scientific or mathematical language, respectively. Note if the student is beginning, developing, or proficient in the associated box under their name. You may wish to attach work samples as evidence of your observations when appropriate, or note that a behavior was not observed during the observational period. You may wish to use this tool as a form of progress monitoring by completing observations on a regular basis.

Individual Conversations

Beyond observing, you can engage in more purposeful analysis of individual students' academic language skills by engaging in one-on-one conversations with students. In these conversations, you can invite the student to use academic language for a variety of purposes with and without teacher scaffolding. For example, engage in a conversation that requires asking and answering questions, invite the student to share a narrative, and ask for an explanation for an idea they share. Ideally, this conversation will be around an academic topic (e.g., a building they have constructed, a book they are reading, an art project, or how they solved a math puzzle). We recommend audio- or video-recording these conversations. Examine the variety of precise academic vocabulary the child uses, with or without you modeling the terms. Explore the length and complexity of the child's utterances, such as whether they use complete sentences with multiple clauses. Taking this zoomed-in look at your students with a "language lens" is a valuable and authentic way to assess the student's academic language use while also building a relationship with the student. Following is a brief excerpt from an individual teacher–student conversation with a 1st-grader during independent reading. The notes in italics are the teacher's reflections on the student's academic language usage.

> *Teacher:* What kinds of books have you read?
> *Treyvon:* Different ones, I've gotten catched up. I just today read *Junie B. Jones Toothless Wonder*. Four chapters and two pages. *[Mix of complete sentences and fragments. Names title of book and uses specific reading-related vocabulary (chapters, pages).]*
> *Teacher:* Wow, did you read that all by yourself?
> *Treyvon:* Yes, I didn't read all of the words. I read the words I knew, pretty much all of them. *[Uses multiple clauses for complex sentences.]*
> *Teacher:* Okay, so you read *Junie B Jones*, would you recommend that book to a friend? Would that be a book you'd share with a friend?
> *Treyvon:* I . . . yeah. *[Answers questions with a mix of brief and extended responses.]*
> *Teacher:* Why, what do you like about it?
> *Treyvon:* I love her. She's super funny. *[Provides information, one simple reason as an explanation.]*

Drawn and Written Artifacts

In addition to language samples, written language artifacts can provide an additional lens into students' academic language competence. Even for emergent writers, a writing sample can give you information about the students' understanding of academic discourse. For example, if a prekindergarten student draws pictures to capture a sequence of events, they are demonstrating an understanding of narrative structure and sequencing. Older students who are mastering conventional writing skills may be able to use academic vocabulary and syntax in their writing, while also accomplishing discourse tasks such as argumentation or explanation. Careful examination of a collection of written artifacts composed for a variety of purposes will give a more complete picture of a student's competence with using academic language in writing.

Assessing ELLs

For ELLs, authentic assessment is especially critical. Anecdotal observations, checklists, and language samples can all be used informally. A collection of performance-based assessments across multiple settings and/or written artifacts can form a portfolio to represent your ELL students' competence with academic language. This information should be examined in tandem with knowledge about your student's language background, and consideration of where the student is in their acquisition of English as an additional language (see Chapter 3). Existing informal assessment checklists, rubrics, and other tools are available at Colorin' Colorado, Reading A-Z, and other websites (see Appendix E). Many early childhood programs and public school systems provide their own resources for assessing English learners in the classroom. Consult with your administration and collaborate with ELL teachers to assess your multilingual students.

FORMAL ASSESSMENTS

Formal assessments also play an important role in assessing academic language. These can aid in collecting systematic data at the classroom, school or program, and district or agency level. While formal assessments provide the benefit of being validated and allowing for group comparisons, they also have limitations in terms of authenticity, time and effort for delivery, cost, and the ability to capture students' competence with academic language across a variety of contexts. Formal assessments should be used in tandem with other sources of information.

Many formal, standardized language assessments focus exclusively on one aspect of language, such as academic vocabulary or syntax. However, recent research has led to some promising developments in creating valid assessments of academic language. The most extensive effort has been from Paola Uccelli et al. (2015a) to develop and validate the Core Academic Language Skills (CALS) assessment for research purposes. This line of research has helped to further define the construct of academic language and contribute a better understanding of how academic language develops over time for students from various backgrounds. The CALS framework highlights the academic language skills most associated with school success (Uccelli et al., 2015a). The CALS assessment is reliable and validated as able to predict reading comprehension (Uccelli & Phillips Galloway, 2017; Uccelli et al., 2015a, 2015b). It has not yet been validated with students younger than 4th grade, although future adaptations may prove useful for early childhood students.

ASSESSING CLASSROOM SUPPORT

Extensive research has associated the quality of the early childhood classroom language environment with students' language growth and related future academic success. For example, Justice et al. (2018) examined features of the preschool classroom language environment and found that teachers' use of communication-facilitating strategies was associated with children's vocabulary growth from preschool to kindergarten. Similarly, Cabell et al. (2015) found that extended, strategic teacher–child conversations in preschool classrooms predicted students' vocabulary growth over the course of the school year. Huttenlocher et al. (2002) examined linguistic input and children's development of syntax and found that preschool teachers' use of complex syntax predicted their students' growth in syntax over the school year.

These findings underscore the importance of examining the early childhood classroom environment and teacher support for academic language. As a teacher, you may self-assess your support for academic language in your classroom and/or work with colleagues to collectively improve academic language support within your team or school. It is necessary to have tools to examine the classroom environment and teaching practices related to academic language. These measures may inform professional development, including coaching, focused on academic language.

Tools for Observing the Classroom

A few tools are available to assess your own classroom for academic language supports and/or work with a peer or coach to have a colleague examine your language supports and provide you some data for your own professional growth.

One helpful tool, particularly if your classroom includes ELLs, is the Sheltered Instruction Observation Protocol (SIOP) (Echevarría et al., 2017). This well-known protocol can drive instruction and planning and may also be used in your self-assessment or observation of other teachers. The SIOP model was designed to support a sheltered English instruction model for multilingual students, emphasizing instruction in the second language with embedded supports for language access and acquisition across content areas. SIOP-based instruction has been implemented in K–12 classrooms. The SIOP focuses on the language supports in a lesson, including planning language objectives for each lesson, embedding comprehensible input into the lesson, and promoting interaction among students. This tool can not only drive planning and instruction, but also allow you to self-assess or have a colleague assess your supports for academic language that benefit not only ELLs but all of your students.

Many other validated classroom observational tools aim to capture the quality of the classroom environment for language and related instructional elements (e.g., literacy, interactions). A few of these commonly used for examining the quality of the early childhood classrooms include the

Early Language and Literacy Classroom Observation measures (ELLCO) (Smith et al., 2008) and the Classroom Assessment Scoring System measures (CLASS) (Pianta et al., 2007). These tools offer a lot in terms of reliability and validity and are frequently used for research or program improvement purposes. However, they are not specifically designed for assessing classroom support for *academic* language and capture much broader aspects of classroom instructional quality.

Tools for Observing Teacher Practice

The need to examine academic language supports in classrooms has led to the development of a tool for observing teacher practice related to academic language. The Academic Language Observation Tool (ALOT) (Grifenhagen, 2016) quantifies the instances of support for academic language within a given lesson or instructional period (see Appendix B). The ALOT collects information about the instances of academic language teaching or support across the three levels of academic language (vocabulary, syntax, and discourse), and comprehensive academic language teaching such as an explicit focus on metalinguistic knowledge. The ALOT has been piloted in pre-K classrooms. While this tool was developed for research purposes, it may be useful in focusing your attention on your academic language supports and tracking how these grow over time. It is best used by an observer who can capture your teaching practice, so it may be useful to have a coach or peer observe to collect these data. You may also self-evaluate your instruction by capturing video-recorded lessons and scoring your academic language support using this tool; this reflective exercise itself can be helpful in your continued growth in support for academic language across your curriculum.

While the ALOT takes a quantitative approach to examining teacher support for academic language, another approach to examining classroom support for academic language is more qualitative and captures both what the teacher and the students are doing with academic language in the classroom. The Academic Language Implementation Assessment (ALIA) (Academic Language Coaching Team, 2016) was developed by a team of academic language coaches working in elementary schools for coaching purposes, but may also be used for self-assessment. This rubric-based assessment (see Appendix C) examines the quality of the academic language environment in the classroom. It can be used as a "snapshot" for individual lessons or to track progress in academic language support over time. It focuses on the language practices the teacher is facilitating and the language students are using. The ALIA has been piloted in elementary classrooms and helped support teacher reflection and contributed to professional development experiences.

CONCLUSION

Whether you are assessing your young students' developing mastery of academic language skills or your own support for academic language, these efforts will help you grow as a teacher of academic language. Academic language assessment should be formative and informative, helping you to both grow as a teacher and differentiate your instruction for your students to ensure they have the academic language foundations for success in literacy, other content areas, and their academic careers. Academic language is not the end goal of instruction in early childhood classrooms. Rather, you are building a foundation to allow your students to access and communicate content, read and write for academic purposes, and fully participate in academic discourse in your classroom and beyond.

Observing Academic Language in Science and Mathematics

Observing Academic Language in Science

	Student Name/Date	Student Name/Date	Student Name/Date
Student understands scientific vocabulary in oral conversations			
Student produces scientific vocabulary in oral conversations			
Student is able to produce an argument			
Student is able to provide claims or evidence to support argument			
Student uses complex syntax in speaking			
Student talks like a scientist			
Student uses appropriate visual representations/symbols			
Student understands scientific metaphor			
Student makes scientific predictions			
Student records scientific data			
Student makes lists			
Student communicates solutions (oral or in writing)			
Student summarizes scientific findings			

Beginning—Student rarely, if ever, displays the behavior with or without support.
Developing—Student uses the behavior on occasion, but not consistently. Some errors in usage may be present. Student may require support.
Proficient—Student consistently uses or understands the behavior. Rarely are errors present. No support is needed.

Observing Academic Language in Mathematics

	Student Name/Date	Student Name/Date	Student Name/Date
Student understands mathematical vocabulary in oral conversations			
Student produces mathematical vocabulary in oral conversations			
Student is able to produce an argument or explanation			
Student is able to provide claims or evidence to support argument or explanation			
Student uses complex syntax in speaking			
Student talks like a mathematician			
Student uses appropriate visual representations or symbols			
Student "translates" word problems to equations			
Student "translates" equations to mathematical language			
Student explains solution to problem (oral/written)			
Student engages in discourse community			
Student understands mathematical language in read-alouds			

Beginning—Student rarely, if ever, displays the behavior with or without support.

Developing—Student uses the behavior on occasion, but not consistently. Some errors in usage may be present. Student may require support.

Proficient—Student consistently uses or understands the behavior. Rarely are errors present. No support is needed.

Academic Language Observation Tool (ALOT)

ACTIVITY

Activity/Lesson: _____   Number of Students Present at Start: _____

Start: _____   End: _____

ACTIVITY CHARACTERISTICS

Content/Subject Areas (choose one):

- ☐ Reading
- ☐ Writing
- ☐ Math
- ☐ Science
- ☐ Social Studies
- ☐ Art
- ☐ Engineering
- ☐ Physical Education
- ☐ Other (specify) _____

Grouping (check all that apply):

- ☐ Whole Class
- ☐ Small Group
- ☐ Individual

Student Discourse Opportunities (check all that apply):

- ☐ Whole Class Discussion
- ☐ Small Group Discussion
- ☐ Pair/Partner Talk

Texts (if applicable):

Title _____

- ☐ Narrative
- ☐ Informational
- ☐ Opinion
- ☐ Other genre
  (specify)_____

Language Objective (check all that apply):

- ☐ Written/Displayed
- ☐ Stated Verbally

Technology (check all that apply):

- ☐ Computer
- ☐ Tablet
- ☐ Smartboard
- ☐ Other (specify)

  _____

Assessment (check all that apply):

- ☐ Formal
- ☐ Informal

Language Domains [Teacher] (check all that apply):

- ☐ Reading
- ☐ Writing
- ☐ Speaking
- ☐ Listening
- ☐ Visually Representing

Language Domains [Students] (check all that apply):

- ☐ Reading
- ☐ Writing
- ☐ Speaking
- ☐ Listening
- ☐ Visually Representing

ACADEMIC LANGUAGE CONTENT SUPPORT/INSTRUCTION

Add/repeat rows to the tables below as needed

Discourse Functions:

Function	Strategies	Function	Strategies
	☐ Explicit Instruction ☐ Modeling ☐ Structure/Sentence Frames ☐ Practice/Application ☐ Feedback ☐ Other:		☐ Explicit Instruction ☐ Modeling ☐ Structure/Sentence Frames ☐ Practice/Application ☐ Feedback ☐ Other:

Vocabulary Instruction:

Word	Strategies	Word	Strategies
	☐ Define ☐ Verbal information ☐ Nonverbal information ☐ Word Study ☐ Practice/Application ☐ Feedback ☐ Other:		☐ Define ☐ Verbal information ☐ Nonverbal information ☐ Word Study ☐ Practice/Application ☐ Feedback ☐ Other:

Syntax Instruction:

Sentence/Phrase	Strategies
	☐ Explicit Instruction ☐ Modeling ☐ Translate/Recast ☐ Feedback ☐ Other:

Other Language Teaching:

Notes	Focus
	☐ Metalinguistic ☐ Dialect/Language Variation ☐ First Language/Cognates ☐ Other:

Academic Language Implementation Assessment (ALIA)

Directions: Review the item descriptors. As you move across each row, check each descriptor that applies.

A level is considered "reached" when all descriptors in a column, and all previous columns, are checked.

Item	Pre-implementation = 0	Emerging/ Developing = 1 (Physical Environment)	Expanding = 2 (Teacher Behaviors)	Optimizing = 3 (Student Behaviors)	Rating
Classroom rules/routines/ procedures	☐ Classroom expectations are not yet displayed.	☐ Classroom expectations are prominently displayed. ☐ Text is large enough to be seen from all parts of room. ☐ Displayed expectations are supported by nonlinguistic representations.	☐ Teacher maintains, actively refers to displayed expectations. ☐ Teacher holds students accountable to displayed expectations.	☐ Students independently follow expectations. ☐ Students hold each other accountable to displayed expectations.	
Norms/contract for respectful and purposeful classroom interactions (speaking and listening)	☐ Norms for respectful and purposeful classroom interactions are not yet accessible.	☐ Norms for respectful and purposeful classroom speaking and listening interactions are accessible. ☐ Text is large enough to be seen from all parts of the classroom, or provided as personal student resource. ☐ Norms are supported by nonlinguistic representations.	☐ Teacher maintains, actively refers to norms. ☐ Teacher holds students accountable to displayed listening and speaking norms for respectful and purposeful classroom interactions. ☐ Teacher maintains structures that support student interaction such as purposeful groupings.	☐ Students independently follow norms. ☐ Students hold each other accountable to listening and speaking norms for respectful and purposeful classroom interactions.	

Effective and flexible collaborative spaces	☐ Flexible collaborative spaces are not yet defined or observable.	☐ Flexible collaborative spaces that promote pair work, small-group work, and whole-group work are observable.	☐ Teacher actively promotes the use of flexible collaborative spaces. ☐ Teacher plans intentional opportunities for students to interact in pairs, small groups, and whole group.	☐ Students interact in flexible collaborative spaces, independently attending to norms of those spaces. ☐ When provided the opportunity, students self-select appropriate collaborative space for work.
Appropriate and relevant language supports (e.g., realia, manipulatives, sentence frames, talk stems, instructional word walls, graphic organizers, anchor charts, work/product exemplars)	☐ Language supports are not yet evident or observable.	☐ Appropriate and relevant language supports are accessible in a variety of forms.	☐ Teacher provides explicit instruction on how to access appropriate and relevant language supports. ☐ Teacher explicitly directs students to use appropriate and relevant language supports.	☐ Students access, utilize, and/or seek appropriate and relevant language supports as needed.
Language outcomes and objectives	☐ Language objectives are not yet displayed or observable.	☐ Language objectives are prominently displayed.	☐ Teacher intentionally plans for specific language outcomes and objectives. ☐ Teacher refers to language objectives during the lesson. ☐ Teacher provides activities that promote the acquisition of stated language objectives.	☐ Students are aware of and can verbalize stated language objectives. ☐ Students demonstrate progress toward the planned language outcome.

(*Continued*)

Item	Pre-implementation = 0	Emerging/ Developing = 1 (Physical Environment)	Expanding = 2 (Teacher Behaviors)	Optimizing = 3 (Student Behaviors)	Rating
Data collection and goal setting	☐ Academic language data is not yet being collected.	☐ Data that informs the development of academic language is being collected for this classroom.	☐ Teacher utilizes data to reflect and set professional goals in relation to academic language. ☐ Teacher utilizes data to inform academic language instruction.	☐ Students utilize data to monitor language use, and set language goals.	
Classroom register use	☐ Awareness of language register is not yet evident or observable.	☐ Examples of informal and academic register are displayed or provided as a personal student resource.	☐ Teacher models appropriate register use. ☐ Teacher may explicitly cue for desired register change.	☐ Students independently apply appropriate register. ☐ Students respond to teacher cues about register change.	
Explicit instruction of academic language features (word/phrase, sentence, discourse, function)	☐ Explicit instruction to develop academic language is not yet observable.	☐ Instructional materials support explicit instruction of academic language features.	☐ Teacher provides explicit instruction in order to develop academic language through language features.	☐ Students actively participate in learning, using explicitly taught language features, in order to develop academic language and content knowledge through SWRL.	
Purposeful Interaction	☐ Purposeful and varied student interactions are not yet observable.	☐ Student interaction supports are accessible.	☐ Teacher facilitates purposeful and varied student interactions, with multiple opportunities for practice, in order to develop academic language and content proficiency.	☐ Students actively engage in purposeful and varied interactions (SWRL) in order to communicate their understanding, develop content knowledge, and respond to learning, using explicitly taught language.	

130

Purposeful feedback	☐ Feedback about specific academic language use is not yet provided.	☐ Tools are accessible to monitor/assess appropriate academic language use in the classroom.	☐ Teacher provides appropriate and relevant feedback in response to specific student academic language use and development. ☐ Teacher facilitates use of tools to monitor/assess appropriate academic language use in the classroom.	☐ Students use a self-assessment tool in order to develop and improve their academic language use. ☐ Students use a peer assessment tool in order to develop and improve their use of academic language.
Equitable access	☐ Awareness of equitable practices is not yet evident or observable.	☐ Space and materials for differentiation are evident.	☐ Teacher holds high expectations for rigorous language development for all students. ☐ Teacher provides ongoing opportunities and supports to develop academic language so that students have equitable access to curriculum.	☐ Students are aware of and respect each other's individual language development. ☐ Students are developing confidence in their own language use.
Leadership	☐ Leadership activities in relation to academic language are not yet observable.	☐ The physical classroom environment is utilized as a model classroom for the development of academic language.	☐ Teacher demonstrates leadership by engaging their peers in the learning academic language theory and practice.	☐ Students hold themselves and peers accountable to rigorous academic language use.

Created by WCPSS Title I Academic Language Coaches (2016, revised 2017).

Children's Literature for Building Academic Language

Anzaldua, G. (1997). *Friends from the other side*. Children's Book Press.

Barnes, D. (2017). *Crown: An ode to the fresh cut*. Agate Publishing.

Barnes, D. (2020). *I am every good thing*. Nancy Paulsen Books.

Burton, V. L. (1939). *Mike Mulligan and his steam shovel*. HMH Books for Young Readers.

Dawson, K. (2015). *The king cake baby*. Pelican Books.

Díaz, J. (2019). *Islandborn*. Dial Books.

Diesen, D., & Hanna, D. (2008). *The pout-pout fish*. Farrar, Straus, Giroux.

Elya, S. M. (2017). *La princesa and the pea*. G. P. Putnam's Sons Books for Young Readers.

Falconer, I. (2000). *Olivia*. Antheneum Books for Young Readers.

Fox, M. (1984). *Wilfrid Gordon McDonald Partridge*. Omnibus Books.

Ginsbury, M. (1998). *Two greedy bears*. Aladdin.

Henkes, K. (2011). *Little white rabbit*. HarperCollins.

Highway, T. (2019). *Dragonfly kites*. Fifth House Publishers.

Hutchins, P. (1967). *Rosie's walk*. Macmillan.

Johnson, C. (1955). *Harold and the purple crayon*. Harper & Brothers.

Keats, E. J. (1962). *The snowy day*. Penguin Young Readers Group.

Kosara, T. (2012). *Hibernation*. Scholastic.

Lin, J. (2019). *Chinese New Year wishes*. Independently published.

Maret, S. (2017). *The cloud artist*. The Roadrunner Press.

May, E. (2013). *Albert is not scared*. Kane Press.

May, E. (2013). *Albert's bigger than big idea*. Kane Press.

Medina, M. (2015). *Mango, abuela, and me*. Candlewick Press.

Medina, M. (2019). *Juana and Lucas*. Candlewick Press.

Mitton, T., & Chapman, L. (2009). *Gnash, gnaw, dinosaur! Prehistoric poems with lift-the-flap surprises!* Kingfisher Publishing.

Mora, P. (2008). *Book fiesta*. HarperCollins.

Morales, Y. (2015). *Niño wrestles the world*. Square Fish.

Murphy, S. J. (1997). *Just enough carrots*. HarperCollins.

Patel, M. (2019). *Priya dreams of marigolds and masala*. Beaver's Pond Press.

Podendorf, I. (1970). *Many is how many? Stepping into science*. Children's Press.

Polacco, P. (1994). *Pink and say*. Philomel Books.

Polacco, P. (1998). *Chicken Sunday*. Puffin Books.

Raschka, C. (1993). *Yo! Yes?* Scholastic.

Robert, N. (2002). *The swirling hijaab*. Mantra Lingua.

Ruurs, M. (2016). *Stepping stones: A refugee family's journey*. Orca Book Publishers.

Rylant, C. (1993). *When I was young in the mountains*. Puffin Books.

Slobodkina, E. (1940). *Caps for sale*. HarperCollins.

Smalls, I. (2004). *Don't say ain't*. Charlesbridge.

Nieminen, L. (2017). *Tacos! An interactive recipe book*. Phaidon Publishing.

Thompkins-Bigelow, J. (2020). *Your name is a song*. The Innovation Press.

Wing, N. (1996). *Jalapeño bagels*. Antheneum Books for Young Readers.

Woodson, J. (2012). *Each kindness*. Nancy Paulsen Books.

Digital Resources

Chapter 7

Resource for teaching kids about nutrition

- USDA's Kids' Corner: https://www.nutrition.gov/topics/nutrition-age /children/kids-corner

Lists of narrative writing mentor texts

- We Are Teachers: https://www.weareteachers.com/mentor-texts -narrative-writing/
- Reading Rockets: https://www.readingrockets.org/article/inviting -personal-narratives-classroom

Read-aloud poetry

- The Children's Poetry Archive: https://childrens.poetryarchive.org

Chapter 8

Songs that cover academic content and involve academic vocabulary and complex syntax

- PBS KIDS *Nature Cat*: https://pbskids.org/naturecat/
- GoNoodle: https://gonoodle.com

Chapter 9

Cognates for English language learners

- The Science Toolkit: https://www.thesciencetoolkit.com/wp-content /uploads/2015/10/04_Cognates-for-Science.pdf

Examples of scientific word walls

- The Science Toolkit Facebook page: https://www.facebook.com/pg /thesciencetoolkit/photos.

Lists of STEM books and resources for creating text sets

- NSTA: https://my.nsta.org/resource/2419

Graphic organizers

- Science A-Z: https://www.sciencea-z.com/main/resourcetype/type
  /graphic-organizers

Chapter 10

Searchable database of books with mathematical language

- Reading Rockets: https://www.readingrockets.org/bookfinder

Mathematical images

- Estimation 180: https://estimation180.com
- Provides images of items (bowls of coins, jars of jelly beans) that
  encourage students to estimate how many are present. Builds number
  sense and mathematical thinking through justifying responses and
  making a mathematical argument.
- Number Talk Images: http://ntimages.weebly.com
- Presents images of items (rows of cupcakes, LEGOs™, tiles) and asks
  students to determine how many are present. Students must present
  their justification for their response. May incorporate mathematical
  vocabulary (row, column, tens, ones).
- Which One Doesn't Belong?: https://wodb.ca
- Presents sets of four images where students must determine which one
  doesn't belong based on their criteria. Students should use academic
  vocabulary to categorize the items and create an argument with
  justification for their selection. Includes shapes, numbers, and graphs.

Chapter 11

Assessment resources for English language learners

- Colorin' Colorado: https://www.colorincolorado.org/using-informal
  -assessment-classroom
- Reading A-Z: https://www.readinga-z.com/ell/ell-assessments
- IES Practice Guide: https://ies.ed.gov/ncee/wwc/PracticeGuide/6

References

Academic Language Coaching Team 2016 (Carr, M., Gilliam, A., Jones, A., Logan, S., Owen, P., Randby, L., Webb, B., & Zawada, D.), Title I Department, Wake County Public School System (2016). *Academic language implementation assessment*. Author.

Adger, C. T., Wolfram, W., & Christian, D. (2014). Dialect awareness for students. In *Dialects in schools and communities* (pp. 163–198). Routledge.

Administration for Children and Families. (2007). *Head Start Act*. U.S. Department of Health and Human Services, Administration for Children and Families, Head Start Program. https://whsaonline.org/wp-content/uploads/2018/03/HS_Act_2007.pdf

Anderson, R. C., & Freebody, P. (1981). Vocabulary knowledge. In J. T. Guthrie (Ed.), *Comprehension and teaching research reviews* (pp. 77–117). International Reading Association.

Bailey, A. L., & Butler, F. A. (2003). *An evidentiary framework for operationalizing academic language for broad application to K–12 education: A design document*. https://cresst.org/wp-content/uploads/R611.pdf

Barnes, E. M., & Dickinson, D. K. (2017). The relationship of academic language and vocabulary growth of children in Head Start preschool classrooms. *Early Education and Development, 28*(7), 794–809. https://doi.org/10.1080/10409289.2017.1340069

Barnes, E. M., & Dickinson, D. K. (2018). Relationships among teachers' use of mental state verbs and children's vocabulary growth. *Early Education and Development, 29*(3), 307–323. https://doi.org/10.1080/10409289.2018.1440844

Barnes, E. M., Dickinson, D. K., & Grifenhagen, J. F. (2017). The role of teachers' comments during book reading in children's vocabulary growth. *The Journal of Educational Research, 110*(5), 515–527.

Barnes, E. M., Grifenhagen, J. F., & Dickinson, D. K. (2016). Academic language in early childhood classrooms. *The Reading Teacher, 70*(1), 39–48. https://doi.org/10.1002/trtr.1463

Barnes, E. M., Grifenhagen, J. F., & Dickinson, D. K. (2020). Mealtimes in Head Start pre-k classrooms: Examining language-promoting opportunities in a hybrid space. *Journal of Child Language, 47*, 337–357. https://doi.org/10.1017/S0305000919000199

Barnes, E. M., & Oliveira, A. W. (2018). Teaching scientific metaphors through informational text read-alouds. *The Reading Teacher, 71*(4), 463–472. https://doi.org/10.1002/trtr.1634

Barnes, E., & Puccioni, J. (2017). Shared book reading and preschool children's academic achievement: Evidence from the Early Childhood Longitudinal Study—Birth cohort. *Infant and Child Development, 26*(6), e2035. https://doi.org/10.1002/icd.2035

Barnes, E. M., & Stephens, S. J. (2019). Vocabulary instruction and support through mathematics curricula. *The Curriculum Journal, 30*(3), 322–341. https://doi.org/10.1080/09585176.2019.1614470

Baumann, J. F., & Graves, M. F. (2010). What is academic vocabulary? *Journal of Adolescent & Adult Literacy, 54*(1), 4–12.

Beals, D. E. (1993). Explanations in low-income families' mealtime conversations. *Applied Psycholinguistics, 14,* 489–513.

Beals, D. E. (1997). Sources of support for learning words in conversation: Evidence from Mealtimes. *Journal of Child Language, 14,* 673–94.

Beals, D. E. (2001). Eating and reading: Links between family conversations with preschoolers and later language and literacy. In D. K. Dickinson & P. O. Tabors (Eds.), *Beginning literacy with language* (pp. 75–92). Paul H. Brookes.

Beck, I. L., & McKeown, M. G. (2001). Text talk: Capturing the benefits of read-aloud experiences for young children. *The Reading Teacher, 55*(1), 10–20.

Biemiller, A., & Slonim, N. (2001). Estimating root word vocabulary growth in normative and advantaged populations: Evidence for a common sequence of vocabulary acquisition. *Journal of Educational Psychology, 93*(3), 489–520. https://doi.org/10.1037/0022-0663.93.3.498

Bond, M. A., & Wasik, B. A. (2009). Conversation stations: Promoting language development in young children. *Early Childhood Education Journal, 36*(6), 467–473. https://doi.org/10.1007/s10643-009-0310-7

Britsch, S. (2019). Exploring science visually: Science and photography with pre-kindergarten children. *Journal of Early Childhood Literacy, 19*(1), 55–81. https://doi.org/10.1177/1468798417700704

Brysbaert, M., Warriner, A. B., & Kuperman, V. (2014). Concreteness ratings for 40 thousand generally known English word lemmas. *Behavior Research Methods, 46*(3), 904–911. https://doi.org/10.3758/s13428-013-0403-5

Bunch, G. C. (2013). Pedagogical language knowledge: Preparing mainstream teachers for English learners in the new standards era. *Review of Research in Education, 37,* 298–341.

Cabell, S. Q., Justice, L. M., McGinty, A. S., DeCoster, J., & Forston, L. D. (2015). Teacher–child conversations in preschool classrooms: Contributions to children's vocabulary development. *Early Childhood Research Quarterly, 30,* 80–92.

Carey, S. (2010). Beyond fast mapping. *Language learning and development: The official Journal of the Society for Language Development, 6*(3), 184–205. https://doi.org/10.1080/15475441.2010.484379

Carrier, S. J., & Grifenhagen, J. F. (2020). Academic vocabulary support for elementary science pre-service teachers. *Journal of Science Teacher Education, 31*(2), 115–133. https://doi.org/10.1080/1046560X.2019.1666631

Cazden, C. (2001). *Classroom discourse.* Heineman.

Cazden, C. (2002). A descriptive study of six high school Puente classrooms. *Educational Policy, 16*(4), 496–521. https://doi.org/10.117/0895904802016004003

Cervetti, G. N., Wright, T. S., & Hwang, H. (2016). Conceptual coherence, comprehension, and vocabulary acquisition: A knowledge effect? *Reading and Writing, 29*(4), 761–779. https://doi.org/10.1007/s11145-016-9628-x

Chamot, A. U., & O'Malley, J. M. (1994). *The CALLA handbook: Implementing the cognitive academic language learning approach.* Addison-Wesley.

Conley, D. T. (2014). Common Core: Development and substance and commentaries. *Social Policy Report, 28*(2), 1–22. https://doi.org/10.1002/j.2379-3988.2014.tb00079.x

Cummins, J. (1979). Cognitive academic language proficiency, linguistic interdependence, the optimum age question and some other matters. *Working Papers on Bilingualism, 19,* 121–129.

Cummins, J. (1981). The role of primary language development in promoting educational success for language minority students. In California State Department of Education (Ed.), *Schooling and language minority students: A theoretical framework.* Evaluation, Dissemination and Assessment Center, California State University, Los Angeles.

Cunningham, P. M., & Cunningham, J. W. (1992). Making Words: Enhancing the invented spelling-decoding connection. *The Reading Teacher, 46*(2), 106–115.

Daniels, H. (2002). *Literature circles: Voice and choice in book clubs and reading groups.* Stenhouse Publishers.

Deacon, S. H., & Kieffer, M. (2018). Understanding how syntactic awareness contributes to reading comprehension: Evidence from mediation and longitudinal models. *Journal of Educational Psychology, 110*(1), 72–86. https://doi.org/10.1037/edu0000198

Degé, F., & Schwarzer, G. (2011). The effect of a music program on phonological awareness in preschoolers. *Frontiers in Psychology, 2*(124), 1–7. https://doi.org/10.3389/fpsyg.2011.00124

Delpit, L., & Dowdy, J. K. (Eds.). (2008). *The skin that we speak: Thoughts on language and culture in the classroom.* The New Press.

Dickinson, D. K., Collins, M. F., Nesbitt, K., Toub, T. S., Hassinger-Das, B., Hadley, E. B., Hirsh-Pasek, K., & Golinkoff, R. M. (2019). Effects of teacher-delivered book reading and play on vocabulary learning and self-regulation among low-income preschool children. *Journal of Cognition and Development, 20*(2), 136–164. https://doi.org/10.1080/15248372.2018.1483373

Dickinson, D. K., Hofer, K. G., Barnes, E. M., & Grifenhagen, J. F. (2014). Examining teachers' language in Head Start classrooms from a systemic linguistics approach. *Early Childhood Research Quarterly, 29*(3), 231–244. https://doi.org/10.1016/j.ecresq.2014.02.006

Dickinson, D. K., McCabe, A., & Sprague, K. (2003). Teacher Rating of Oral Language and Literary Development (TROLL): Individualizing early literacy instruction with a standards-based rating tool. *The Reading Teacher, 56,* 554–569.

Dickinson, D. K., & Porche, M. V. (2011). Relation between language experiences in preschool classrooms and children's kindergarten and fourth-grade language and reading abilities. *Child Development, 82*(3), 870–886. https://doi.org/10.1111/j.1467-8624.2011.01576.x

Dickinson, D. K., & Smith, M. W. (1994). Long-term effects of preschool teachers' book readings on low-income children's vocabulary and story comprehension. *Reading Research Quarterly, 29*(2), 105–122.

Dickinson, D. K., & Tabors, P. O. (Eds.). (2001). *Beginning literacy with language: Young children learning at home and school.* Paul H. Brookes.

Diesen, D. (2008). *The pout-pout fish.* Scholastic, Inc.

Dyson, A. H., & Smitherman, G. (2009). The right (write) start: African American language and the discourse of sounding right. *Teachers College Record, 111*(4), 973–998.

Echevarría, J., Vogt, M. E., & Short, D. J. (2017). *Making content comprehensible for English learners: The SIOP model* (5th ed.). Pearson.

Fang, Z. (2006). The language demands of science reading in middle school. *International Journal of Science Education, 28*(5), 491–520. https://doi.org/10.1080/09500060690500033092

Farrow, J., Wasik, B. A., & Hindman, A. H. (2020). Exploring the unique contributions of teachers' syntax to preschoolers' and kindergarteners' vocabulary learning. *Early Childhood Research Quarterly, 51,* 178–190. https://doi.org/10.1016/j.ecresq.2019.08.005

Firmender, J. M., Gavin, M. K., & McCoach, D. B. (2014). Examining the relationship between teachers' instructional practices and students' mathematics achievement. *Journal of Advanced Academics, 25*(3), 214–236. https://doi.org/10.1177/1932202X14538032

Fogel, H., & Ehri, L. C. (2000). Teaching elementary students who speak Black English vernacular to write in standard English: Effects of dialect transformation practice. *Contemporary Educational Psychology, 25*(2), 212–235.

Fox, M. (1984). *Wilfrid Gordon McDonald Partridge.* Omnibus Books.

Frayer, D., Frederick, W. C., & Klausmeier, H. J. (1969). *A schema for testing the level of cognitive mastery.* Wisconsin Center for Education Research.

Gallagher, C. (2016). Socialization to academic language in a kindergarten classroom. *Language and Education, 30*(5), 383–399.

Garcia, O., & Kleifgen, J. (2021). Translanguaging and literacies. *Reading Research Quarterly, 55*(4), 553–571. https://doi.org/10.1002/rrq.286

Golinkoff, R. M., Can, D. D., Soderstrom, M., & Hirsh-Pasek, K. (2015). (Baby)Talk to me: The social context of infant-directed speech and its effects on early language acquisition. *Current Directions in Psychological Science, 24*(5), 339–344. https://doi.org/10.1177/0963721415595345

González, N., Moll, L. C., & Amanti, C. (2006). *Funds of knowledge: Theorizing practices in households, communities, and classrooms*. Routledge.

Goodwin, A., Lipsky, M., & Ahn, S. (2012). Word detectives: Using units of meaning to support literacy. *The Reading Teacher*, 65(7), 461–470. https://doi.org/10.1002/TRTR.01069

Gordon, R. L., Shivers, C. M., Wieland, E. A., Kotz, S. A., Yoder, P. J., & Devin McAuley, J. (2015). Musical rhythm discrimination explains individual differences in grammar skills in children. *Developmental Science, 18*(4), 635–644. https://doi.org/10.1111/desc.12230

Grifenhagen, J. F. (2016, December). *ALOT to measure: Developing an academic language observation tool* [Paper presentation]. Literacy Research Association Annual Meeting, Nashville, TN.

Gutlohn, L., & Bessellieu, F. (2014). *Word ID: Assessment across the content areas*. Academic Therapy Publications.

Hadaway, N. L., Vardell, S. M., & Young, T. A. (2001). Scaffolding oral language development through poetry for students learning English. *The Reading Teacher*, 54(8), 796–806.

Hadley, E. B., Dickinson, D. K., Hirsh-Pasek, K., & Golinkoff, R. M. (2019). Building semantic networks: The impact of a vocabulary intervention on preschoolers' depth of word knowledge. *Reading Research Quarterly, 54*(1), 41–61. https://doi.org/10.1002/rrq.225

Hadley, E. B., Newman, K. M., & Mock, J. (2020). Setting the stage for TALK: Strategies for encouraging language-building conversations. *The Reading Teacher*, 74(1), 39–48. https://doi.org/10.1002/trtr.1900

Halliday, M. A. K. (1978). *Language as social semiotic: The social interpretation of language and meaning*. Hodder Arnold.

Hand, B., Norton-Meier, L. A., Gunel, M., & Akkus, R. (2016). Aligning teaching to learning: A 3-year study examining the embedding of language and argumentation into elementary science classrooms. *International Journal of Science and Mathematics Education, 14*(5), 847–863.

Harris, J., Golinkoff, R., & Hirsh-Pasek, K. (2011). Lessons from the crib to the classroom: How children really learn vocabulary. *Handbook of Early Literacy Research, 3*, 322–336.

Hartman, P., & Machado, E. (2019). Language, race, and critical conversations in a primary-grade writers' workshop. *The Reading Teacher*, 73(3), 313–323.

Hassinger-Das, B., Jordan, N. C., & Dyson, N. (2015). Reading stories to learn math. *The Elementary School Journal, 116*(2), 242–264. https://doi.org/10.1086/683986

Heath, S. B. (1983). *Ways with words: Language, life and work in communities and classrooms*. Cambridge University Press.

Heath, S. B. (2012). *Words at work and play: Three decades in family and community life*. Cambridge University Press.

Heller, V. (2015). Academic discourse practices in action: Invoking discursive norms in mathematics and language lessons. *Linguistics and Education, 31*, 187–206. https://doi.org/10.1016/j.linged.2014.12.003

Hiebert, E. H., Goodwin, A. P., & Cervetti, G. N. (2018). Core vocabulary: Its morphological content and presence in exemplar texts. *Reading Research Quarterly, 53*(1), 29–49. https://doi.org/10.1002/rrq.183

Howe, N., Petrakos, H., Rinaldi, C. M., & LeFebvre, R. (2005). "This is a bad dog, you know . . . ": Constructing shared meanings during sibling pretend play. *Child Development,*76(4),783–794.https://doi.org/10.1111/j.1467-8624.2005.00877.x

Hussar, B., Zhang, J., Hein, S., Wang, K., Roberts, A., Cui, J., Smith, M., Bullock Mann, F., Barmer, A., & Dilig, R. (2020). *The condition of education 2020* (NCES 2020-144). U.S. Department of Education. National Center for Education Statistics. https://nces.ed.gov/pubs2020/2020144.pdf

Huttenlocher, J., Vasilyeva, M., Cymerman, E., & Levine, S. (2002). Language input and child syntax. *Cognitive Psychology, 45*(3), 337–374. https://doi.org/10.1016/S0010-0285(02)00500-5

Jackson, J., & Durham, A. (2016). Planning and using interactive word walls to support science and reading instruction. *Science and Children, 7*, 78–84.

Justice, L. M., Jiang, H., & Strasser, K. (2018). Linguistic environment of preschool classrooms: What dimensions support children's language growth? *Early Childhood Research Quarterly, 42*, 79–92.

Justice, L. M., McGinty, A. S., Zucker, T., Cabell, S. Q., & Piasta, S. B. (2013). Bidirectional dynamics underlie the complexity of talk in teacher–child play-based conversations in classrooms serving at-risk pupils. *Early Childhood Research Quarterly, 28*(3), 496–508. https://doi.org/10.1016/j.ecresq.2013.02.005

Kosara, T. (2012). *Hibernation*. Scholastic.

Lawson-Adams, J., & Dickinson, D. (2020). Sound stories: Using nonverbal sound effects to support English word leaning in first-grade music classrooms. *Reading Research Quarterly, 55*(3), 419–441. https://doi.org/10.1002/rrq.280

Lazaraton, A. (1992). Linking ideas with AND in spoken and written discourse. *International Review of Applied Linguistics, 30*(3), 191–206.

Lemaster, J., & Willett, V. (2019). Pushes, pulls, and playgrounds. *Science & Children, 56*(7) 50–56

Lobeck, A. (2019). Teaching linguistic diversity as the rule rather than the exception. In M. D. Devereaux & C. C. Palmer (Eds.), *Teaching language variation in the classroom: Strategies and models from teachers and linguists*. Routledge.

Lucero, A. (2014). Teachers' use of linguistic scaffolding to support the academic language development of first-grade emergent bilingual students. *Journal of Early Childhood Literacy, 14*(4), 534–561.

Macedo, A. P. (2011). *The development of children's argument skills*. Royal Holloway University of London.

Machado, E., & Hartman, P. (2019). Translingual writing in a linguistically diverse primary classroom. *Journal of Literacy Research, 51*(4), 480–503.

Maguire, M. J., Hirsh-Pasek, K., & Golinkoff, R. (2006). A unified theory of word learning: Putting verb acquisition in context. In K. Hirsh-Pasek & R. M. Golinkoff (Eds.), *Action meets word: How children learn verbs*. Oxford University Press.

Mancilla-Martinez, J., & Lesaux, N. K. (2010). Predictors of reading comprehension for struggling readers: The case of Spanish-speaking language minority learners. *Journal of Educational Psychology, 102*(3), 701–711. https://doi.org/10.1037/a0019135

Manyak, P. C. (2010). Vocabulary instruction for English learners: Lessons from MCVIP. *The Reading Teacher, 64*(2), 143–146. https://doi.org/10.1598/RT.64.2.10

Marulis, L. M., & Neuman, S. B. (2010). The effects of vocabulary intervention on young children's word learning: A meta-analysis. *Review of Educational Research, 80*(3), 300–335. https://doi.org/10.3102/0034654310377087

Massey, S. L., Pence, K. L., Justice, L. M., & Bowles, R. P. (2008). Educators' use of cognitively challenging questions in economically disadvantaged preschool classroom contexts. *Early Education and Development, 19*(2), 340–360.

Méndez Barletta, L. M. (2008). Teachers' differential treatment of culturally and linguistically diverse students during sharing time. *Colorado Research in Linguistics, 21*.

Menon, V., & Levitin, D. J. (2005). The rewards of music listening: Response and physiological connectivity of the mesolimbic system. *NeuroImage, 28*(1), 175–184. https://doi.org/10.1016/j.neuroimage.2005.05.053

Michaels, S. (1981). "Sharing time": Children's narrative styles and differential access to literacy. *Language in Society, 10*(3), 423–442. https://doi.org/10.1017/S0047404500008861

Michaels, S., O'Connor, C., & Resnick, L. B. (2008). Deliberative discourse idealized and realized: Accountable talk in the classroom and in civic life. *Studies in Philosophy and Education, 27*(4), 283–297.

Mitton, T., & Chapman, L. (2009). *Gnash, gnaw, dinosaur! Prehistorical poems with lift-the-flap surprises!* Kingfisher.

Moje, E. B., Dillon, D. R., & O'Brien, D. (2000). Reexamining roles of learner, text, and context in secondary literacy. *Journal of Educational Research, 93*(3), 165–180.

Mokhtari, K., & Thompson, H. B. (2006). How problems of reading fluency and comprehension are related to difficulties in syntactic awareness skills among fifth graders. *Reading Research and Instruction, 46*(1), 73–94. https://doi.org/10.1080/19388070609558461

Moreno, S., Friesen, D., & Bialystok, E. (2011). Effect of music training on promoting preliteracy skills: Preliminary causal evidence. *Music Perception, 29*(2), 165–172. https://doi.org/10.1525/mp.2011.29.2.165

Moritz, C., Yampolsky, S., Papadelis, G., Thomson, J., & Wolf, M. (2012). Links between early rhythm skills, musical training, and phonological awareness. *Reading and Writing: An Interdisciplinary Journal, 26*(5), 739–769. https://doi.org/10.1007/s11145-012-9389-0

Nagy, W., & Townsend, D. (2012). Words as tools: Learning academic vocabulary as language acquisition. *Reading Research Quarterly, 47*, 91–108. https://doi.org/10.1002/RRQ.011

Nation, K., & Snowling, M. J. (2000). Factors influencing syntactic awareness skills in normal readers and poor comprehenders. *Applied Psycholinguistics, 21*(2), 229–241. https://doi.org/10.1017/S0142716400002046

National Council of Teachers of Mathematics. (2014). *Principles to actions: Ensuring mathematical success for all.* Author.

National Governors Association. (2010). *Common Core State Standards.* Author.

Neugebauer, S. R., Gámez, P. B., Coyne, M. D., Cólon, I. T., McCoach, D. B., & Ware, S. (2017). Promoting word consciousness to close the vocabulary gap in young word learners. *The Elementary School Journal, 118*(1), 28–54. https://doi.org/10.1086/692986

Neuman, S. B., & Kaefer, T. (2018). Developing low-income children's vocabulary and content knowledge through a shared book reading program. *Contemporary Educational Psychology, 52,* 15–24. https://doi.org/10.1016/j.cedpsych.2017.12.001

Neuman, S. B., Newman, E. H., & Dwyer, J. (2011). Educational effects of a vocabulary intervention on preschoolers' word knowledge and conceptual development: A cluster-randomized trial. *Reading Research Quarterly, 46*(3), 249–272. https://doi.org/10.1598/RRQ.46.3.3

Neuman, S. B., & Wright, T.S. (2013). *All about words: Increasing vocabulary in the common core classroom, PreK-2.* Teachers College Press.

Newell, C., & Orton, C. (2018). Classroom routines: An invitation to discourse. *Teaching Children Mathematics, 25*(2), 94–102. https://doi.org/10.5951/teacchilmath.25.2.0094

Nicolopoulou, A., Cortina, K. S., Ilgaz, H., Cates Brockmeyer, C., & de Sá, A. (2015). Using a narrative- and play-based activity to promote low-income preschoolers' oral language, emergent literacy, and social competence. *Early Childhood Research Quarterly, 31,* 147–162. https://doi.org/10.1016/j.ecresq.2015.01.006

Nieminen, L. (2017). *Tacos! An interactive recipe book.* Phaidon.

Nippold M. A., Hesketh L. J., Duthie J. K., & Mansfield T. C. (2005). Conversational versus expository discourse. *Journal of Speech, Language, and Hearing Research, 48*(5), 1048–1064. https://doi.org/10.1044/1092-4388(2005/073)

Orosco, M. J. (2014). Word problem strategy for Latino English language learners at risk for math disabilities. *Learning Disability Quarterly, 37*(1), 45–53. https://doi.org/10.1177/0731948713504206

Paris, D., & Alim, H. S. (2014). What are we seeking to sustain through culturally sustaining pedagogy? A loving critique forward. *Harvard Educational Review, 84*(1), 85–100. https://doi.org/10.17763/haer.84.1.982l873k2ht16m77

Patel, A. D. (2008). *Music, language, and the brain.* Oxford University Press.

Paul, R. (1981). Analyzing complex sentence development. In J. F. Miller (Ed.), *Assessing language production in children: Experimental procedures* (pp. 36–40). University Park Press.

Pentimonti, J. M., Zucker, T. A., Justice, L. M., & Kaderavek, J. N. (2010). Informational text use in preschool classroom read-alouds. *The Reading Teacher, 63*(8), 656–665.

Peterson, C., & McCabe, A. (1994). A social interactionist account of developing decontextualized narrative skill. *Developmental Psychology, 30*(6), 937–948. https://doi.org/10.1037/0012-1649.30.6.937

Phillips, B. M. (2014). Promotion of syntactical development and oral comprehension: Development and initial evaluation of a small-group intervention. *Child Language Teaching and Therapy, 30*(1), 63–77. https://doi.org /10.1177/0265659013487742

Pianta, R. C., La Paro, K. M., & Hamre, B. K. (2008). *Classroom Assessment Scoring System™: Manual K-3.* Paul H. Brookes.

Pinker, S. (2013). *Language, cognition, and human nature.* Oxford University Press.

Pollard-Durodola, S., Gonzalez, J., Simmons, D., Taylor, A., Davis, M., & Simmons, L. (2014). Accelerating preschoolers' content vocabulary: Designing a shared book intervention in collaboration with teachers. *NHSA Dialog A Research-to-Practice Journal for the Early Intervention Field, 17*(3). https://www.research gate.net/publication/266968193

Pollard-Durodola, S. D., Gonzalez, J. E., Simmons, D. C., & Simmons, L. E. (2015). *Accelerating language skills and content knowledge through shared book reading.* Paul H. Brookes.

Protacio, M. S., & Edwards, P. A. (2015). Restructuring sharing time for English learners and their parents. *The Reading Teacher, 68*(6), 413–421. https://doi.org /10.1002/trtr.1327

Purpura, D. J., Napoli, A. R., Wehrspann, E. A., & Gold, Z. S. (2017). Causal connections between mathematical language and mathematical knowledge: A dialogic reading intervention. *Journal of Research on Educational Effectiveness, 10*(1), 116–137. https://doi.org/10.1080/19345747.2016.1204639

Reardon, S. F., Valentino, R. A., & Shores, K. A. (2012). Patterns of literacy among U.S. students. *The Future of Children, 22*(2), 17–37. https://doi.org/10.1353/foc .2012.0015

Reaser, J., Adger, C. T., Wolfram, W., & Christian, D. (2017). *Dialects at school: Educating linguistically diverse students.* Taylor & Francis.

Riccomini, P. J., Smith, G. W., Hughes, E. M., & Fries, K. M. (2015). The language of mathematics: The importance of teaching and learning mathematical vocabulary. *Reading & Writing Quarterly, 31*(3), 235–252. https://doi.org/10.1080 /10573569.2015.1030995

Richter, B., & Richter, S. (2000*). Alaska animals—Where do they go at 40 below?* Alaska Children's Books.

Romeo, R. R., Leonard, J. A., Robinson, S. T., West, M. R., Mackey, A. P., Rowe, M. L., & Gabrieli, J. D. E. (2018). Beyond the 30-million-word gap: Children's conversational exposure is associated with language-related brain function. *Psychological Science, 29*(5), 700–710. https://doi.org/10.1177/0956797617742725

Romeo, R. R., Segaran, J., Leonard, J. A., Robinson, S. T., West, M. R., Mackey, A. P., Yendiki, A., Rowe, M. L., & Gabrieli, J. D. E. (2018). Language exposure relates to structural neural connectivity in childhood. *Journal of Neuroscience, 38*(36), 7870–7877. https://doi.org/10.1523/JNEUROSCI.0484-18.2018

Roop, P., & Roop, C. (1998). *If you lived with the Cherokee*. Scholastic, Inc.

Rowe, M. L. (2012). A longitudinal investigation of the role of quantity and quality of child-directed speech in vocabulary development. *Child Development, 83*(5), 1762–1774. https://doi.org/10.1111/j.1467-8624.2012.01805.x

Rowe, M. L. (2013). Decontextualized language input and preschoolers' vocabulary development. *Seminars in Speech and Language, 34*(4), 260–266.

Rowsell, J., Burke, A., Flewitt, R., Liao, H. T., Lin, A., Marsh, J., Mills, K., Prinsloo, M., Rowe, D., & Wohlwend, K. (2016). Humanizing digital literacies: A road trip in search of wisdom and insight. *The Reading Teacher, 70*(1), 121–129.

Sandoval, W. A., Enyedy, N., Redman, E. H., & Xiao, S. (2019). Organising a culture of argumentation in elementary science. *International Journal of Science Education, 41*(13), 1848–1869.

Scheele, A. F., Leseman, P. P., Mayo, A. Y., & Elbers, E. (2012). The relation of home language and literacy to three-year-old children's emergent academic language in narrative and instruction genres. *The Elementary School Journal, 112*(3), 419–444.

Schleppegrell, M. J. (2001). Linguistic features of the language of schooling. *Linguistics and Education, 12*(4), 431–459.

Schleppegrell, M. J. (2004). *The language of schooling: A functional linguistics perspective*. Routledge.

Schleppegrell, M. J. (2007). The linguistic challenges of mathematics teaching and learning: A research review. *Reading & Writing Quarterly, 23*(2), 139–159. https://doi.org/10.1080/10573560601158461

Schleppegrell, M. J. (2012). Academic language in teaching and learning: Introduction to the special issue. *The Elementary School Journal, 112*(3), 409–418.

Share, D. L., & Leikin, M. (2004). Language impairment at school entry and later reading disability: Connections at lexical versus supralexical levels of reading. *Scientific Studies of Reading, 8*(1), 87–110.

Smith, M., Brady, J., & Clark-Chiarelli, N. (2008). *Early Language and Literacy Classroom Observation Tool, K-3* (ELLCO K-3). Brookes.

Snow, C. E. (1983). Linguistic development as related to literacy. *Early Intervention and Culture*, 133–148.

Snow, C. E., & Uccelli, P. (2009). The challenge of academic language. In D. R. Olson & N. Torrance (Eds.), *The Cambridge handbook of literacy* (pp. 112–133). Cambridge University Press.

Soter, A. O., Wilkinson, I. A., Murphy, P. K., Rudge, L., Reninger, K., & Edwards, M. (2008). What the discourse tells us: Talk and indicators of high-level comprehension. *International Journal of Educational Research, 47*(6), 372–391.

Souto-Manning, M. (2013). Competence as linguistic alignment: Linguistic diversities, affinity groups, and the politics of educational success. *Linguistics and Education, 24*(3), 305–315.

Souto-Manning, M. (2016). Honoring and building on the rich literacy practices of young bilingual and multilingual learners. *The Reading Teacher, 70*(3), 263–271.

Storch, S. A., & Whitehurst, G. J. (2002). Oral language and code-related precursors to reading: Evidence from a longitudinal structural model. *Developmental Psychology, 38*(6), 934–947. https://psycnet.apa.org/doi/10.1037/0012-1649.38.6.934

Tomasello, M. (2000). First steps toward a usage-based theory of language acquisition. *Cognitive Linguistics, 11*(1–2). https://doi.org/10.1515/cogl.2001.012

Toub, T. S., Hassinger-Das, B., Nesbitt, K. T., Ilgaz, H., Weisberg, D. S., Hirsh-Pasek, K., Golinkoff, R. M., Nicolopoulou, A., & Dickinson, D. K. (2018). The language of play: Developing preschool vocabulary through play following shared book-reading. *Early Childhood Research Quarterly, 45*, 1–17. https://doi.org/10.1016/j.ecresq.2018.01.010

Uccelli, P., Barr, C. D., Dobbs, C. L., Galloway, E. P., Meneses, A., & Sanchez, E. (2015a). Core Academic Language Skills (CALS): An expanded operational construct and a novel instrument to chart school-relevant language proficiency in per-adolescent and adolescent learners. *Applied Psycholinguistics, 36*(5), 1077–1109.

Uccelli, P., Galloway, E. P., Barr, C. D., Meneses, A., & Dobbs, C. L. (2015b). Beyond vocabulary: Exploring cross-disciplinary academic-language proficiency and its association with reading comprehension. *Reading Research Quarterly, 50*(3), 337–356.

Uccelli, P., & Phillips Galloway, E. (2017). Academic language across content areas: Lessons from an innovative assessment and from students' reflections about language. *Journal of Adolescent & Adult Literacy, 60*(4), 395–404.

van Kleeck, A. (2014). Distinguishing between casual talk and academic talk beginning in the preschool years: An important consideration for speech-language pathologists. *American Journal of Speech-Language Pathology, 23*(4), 724–741.

van Kleeck, A. (2015). The academic talk register: A critical preschool oral language foundation for later reading comprehension. In A. DeBruin-Parecki, A. van Kleeck, & S. B. Gear (Eds.), *Developing early comprehension: Laying the foundation for reading success* (pp. 52–76). Paul H. Brookes.

van Kleeck A., Vander Woude J., & Hammett L. (2006). Fostering literal and inferential language skills in Head Start preschoolers with language impairment using scripted book-sharing discussions. *American Journal of Speech-Language Pathology, 15*(1), 85–95. https://doi.org/10.1044/1058-0360(2006/009)

Vasilyeva, M., Huttenlocher, J., & Waterfall, H. (2006). Effects of language intervention on syntactic skill levels in preschoolers. *Developmental Psychology, 42*(1), 164–174. https://doi.org/10.1037/0012-1649.42.1.164

Vasilyeva, M., & Waterfall, H. (2011). Variability in language development: Relation to socioeconomic status and environmental input. In S. K. Neuman & D. K. Dickinson (Eds.) *Handbook of early literacy research* (Vol. III, pp. 36–48). Guilford.

Vukovic, R. K., & Lesaux, N. K. (2013). The language of mathematics: Investigating the ways language counts for children's mathematical development. *Journal of Experimental Child Psychology, 115*(2), 227–244. https://doi.org/10.1016/j.jecp.2013.02.002

Weizman, Z. O., & Snow, C. E. (2001). Lexical input as related to children's vocabulary acquisition: Effects of sophisticated exposure and support for meaning. *Developmental Psychology, 37*(2), 265–279. https://doi.org/10.1037
   /0012-1649.37.2.265.

Westby, C. E. (1985). Learning to talk-talking to learn: Oral-literate language dif-
   ferences. In C. Simon (Ed.), *Communication skills and classroom success:
   Therapy methodologies for language-learning disabled students* (pp. 182–213).
   College-Hill.

Yopp, R. H., & Yopp, H. K. (2012). Young children's limited and narrow exposure
   to informational text. *The Reading Teacher, 65*(7), 480–490.

Index

abstract academic verbs for instruction, 34

academic definitions, 51–52

academic discourse
contextualization, 53–54
in early childhood classrooms, 56–66
genre, 55–56, 88–89
oral, 55–56, 57–59
patterns of, 57
stance, 54–55
tone, 54
written, 55–56

academic language, 1–4, 42
checklist, 117
children's literature for building, 132–133
development, linguistic diversity and, 25–28
in early childhood classrooms, 4–9
features and descriptions of. *See specific features*
interpersonal language *vs.*, 23
in mathematics, observing, 124
in mealtimes, 69
organization and structure of, 7
in science, observing, 123
teaching with music, 87

Academic Language Implementation Assessment (ALIA), 121, 127–131

Academic Language Observation Tool (ALOT), 121, 125–126

academic register, 1, 18–23
features of, 20–21, 25

academic texts, complex syntax in, 45–46

academic vocabulary, 3, 4, 6–7. *See also* vocabulary
categorizations of, 7, 30–31

content-specific, 90
defined, 6, 30
nonspecialized, 30–31
teaching, 35–40, 89–91
words, 32–35

Academic Word List (AWL), 33

Adger, C. T., 24

adult-child conversations, 15–17

adverbial clause, 44

Ahn, S., 96

Akkus, R., 56

Alim, H. S., 87

Amanti, C., 22

anchor chart, 61

Anderson, R. C., 6, 94

arguments, 57
mathematical, 111–112

artifacts, written language, 118

assessment, language, 114
authentic, 114
classroom support, 119–121
formal, 119
informal. *See* informal assessments
principles of, 114–116
realistic, 115–116

attributive clause, 8

authentic writing, 27–28

Bailey, A. L., 1, 42

Barmer, A., 23

Barnes, E. M., 3, 35, 47, 49, 97, 104, ix, xii, xv, xvi

Barr, C. D., 119, xiii

Basic Interpersonal Communication Skills (BICS), 23

Baumann, J. F., 6, 7

Beals, D. E., 68

Beck, I. L., 56, 61

About the Authors

Erica M. Barnes, PhD, is an associate professor in the Department of Literacy Teaching and Learning at the University of Albany. Her research investigates teacher–child interactions in preschool and early elementary classrooms that promote language and literacy growth, with an emphasis on the developmental trajectories of children with varying levels of language abilities from low-income homes. Her work focuses on developing supports for teachers and professionals working with children in preschool and early childhood classrooms, particularly around teaching academic language and literacy through the content areas. She received her doctorate in development, learning, and diversity from Vanderbilt University's Peabody College and holds a master's degree in literacy and learning disabilities from the University of Michigan. She received the Outstanding Dissertation award from the Early Childhood SIG of AERA in 2015. She is a former teacher, teacher consultant, and progress monitoring specialist.

Jill F. Grifenhagen, PhD, is an assistant professor of literacy education at North Carolina State University. She is a former early elementary classroom teacher and instructional coach. Her research focuses on the role of teachers' talk and instructional practices in early childhood (pre-K–3) classrooms that support young children's vocabulary and academic language learning. She is particularly interested in equity-focused, research–practitioner partnerships to increase learning opportunities for and address the needs of students from underserved communities. To this end, she seeks to develop the best preparation and professional development for teachers to improve language and literacy practices. Her current work is developing literacy-focused induction supports for novice, primary-grade teachers in high-need schools. She takes on leadership roles in early childhood and elementary literacy education at the state level, working with policymakers and practitioners to apply research-based solutions to current educational challenges. Her work has been published in many journals, including *Literacy Research and Instruction, Early Childhood Research Quarterly, The Reading Teacher*, and *Journal of Child Language.*

David K. Dickinson is an endowed chair of education at Vanderbilt University's Peabody College. He received his EdD from Harvard's Graduate School of

Education. He has pursued three lines of inquiry: (1) examining the relationship between language and early reading; (2) studying language environments in classrooms and their impact on language use and learning; and (3) developing methods for supporting language learning of children from low-income homes. He advocates for engaging and intellectually challenging early childhood classrooms, with particular attention to language development. He developed the first widely delivered professional development intervention focusing on language and early literacy, helped develop the research tools used to describe classroom language and literacy environments, helped with the revision of the accreditation standards of NAEYC, and assisted in creating the Early Childhood Generalist certificate for the National Board for Professional Teaching Standards. He has authored more than 120 articles and chapters, coedited three volumes of the *Handbook of Early Literacy,* and coauthored *Opening the World of Learning,* a widely used preschool curriculum. He is the coauthor of *Connecting Through Talk: Nourishing Children's Development With Language.* Currently, he is collaborating with the Video Interaction Project directed by Alan Mendelsohn, which helps parents adopt more responsive conversational methods.

Printed and bound by CPI Group (UK) Ltd, Croydon, CR0 4YY

09/06/2025

14685968-0003